To your

Richard

Marketing Survival Guide

Be Unique, Get Noticed, and Double Your Sales Without Wasting Money On Advertising

Local Business Success Series

Marketing Survival Guide

Be Unique, Get Noticed, and Double Your Sales Without Wasting Money On Advertising

Richard Emmons

Work Smart Press
worksmartpress.com

Published by Work Smart Press
1867 Williams Highway, Suite 250
Grants Pass, OR 97527

Visit the author's website at www.richardemmons.com.

Cover design by Kathleen Emmons, Reality Marketing LLC
Cartoons © Randy Glasbergen, Glasbergen Cartoon Service
Author photograph by Jacquelyn Cease

ISBN: 978-1-970101-00-3 (paperback)

Library of Congress Control Number: 2019903137

This publication is designed to provide accurate and authoritative information in regard to the subject matter covered. It is sold with the understanding that the publisher is not engaged in rendering legal, accounting, or other professional services. If legal advice or other expert assistance is required, the services of a competent professional person should be sought.

The author and publisher are not responsible for the URL's used in this book which may change at any time depending on the website.

To my wife Kathleen, a "match-made-in-heaven" partner in life

Acknowledgments

I want to thank all the people who have taught me marketing and copywriting over the years. I love learning from great teachers who are masters of their craft, whether in person or through webinars, books, newsletters, cassette tapes, CDs, DVDs, or Kindle books.

I want to give a special shout-out to four copywriting and marketing greats who helped me the most when I was starting out. Jay Abraham, Mark Ford (aka Mark Masterson), Bob Bly, and Ted Nicholas are forever carved into my "Marketing Mount Rushmore."

You'll read pithy, pointed, and purposeful quotes in this book from many other people who have helped me along the way.

I also want to thank my marketing consulting clients who paid me to solve their marketing problems. Special thanks to The Boardroom for giving me the opportunity to be the boss and run a brick-and-mortar business.

Finally, special thanks to Constance Frankland for editing my book, Kathleen Emmons for designing the cover, and my beta readers. All offered helpful suggestions to make this a better book for you my readers.

Always be learning and implement what you learn so you can earn from what you learn.

Contents

Preface xiii

Introduction xv

Part 1: Ready, Set, Grow 1

    Introduction to Part 1 3

    Chapter 1 Why You Want Clients, Not Customers 5

    Chapter 2 How To Double Your Business 7

    Chapter 3 Do "Marketing Magic Bullets" Exist? 11

    Chapter 4 Your Marketing Mindset 15

    Chapter 5 80/20 Time Management 19

    Chapter 6 Find More Time For Marketing 21

    Chapter 7 Spend Less Time On Administration 23

    Chapter 8 Spend Less Time On Operations 25

    Chapter 9 Why Multitasking Destroys Productivity 27

    Chapter 10 Five Ways To Work Smarter 29

    Review of Part 1 35

Part 2: Be Unique 37

    Introduction to Part 2 39

    Chapter 11 Your Personal Brand 41

    Chapter 12 Collect Testimonials 43

    Chapter 13 What's a USP? 45

    Chapter 14 Five Steps To a Winning USP 49

    Chapter 15 Your Elevator Pitch 57

    Chapter 16 Write a Biography That Sells 59

    Chapter 17 USP Case Study: Financial Advisor 61

    Chapter 18 USP Case Study: The Boardroom 67

    Chapter 19 Putting Your USP To Work 73

    Review of Part 2 77

Part 3: Get Noticed 79
   Introduction to Part 3 81
   Chapter 20 Get Noticed Without Advertising 83
   Chapter 21 Get Clients With Endorsement Letters 87
   Chapter 22 Effective Advertising 91
   Chapter 23 Image Advertising 95
   Chapter 24 Direct Response Advertising 97
   Chapter 25 The Easiest Way To Fix Your Ads 101
   Chapter 26 Creating Effective Ad Campaigns 103
   Chapter 27 Know Your Market and Define Your Avatar 107
   Chapter 28 Seven Copywriting Basics 111
   Chapter 29 Successful Advertising Formulas 119
   Chapter 30 Grab Attention with Your Headline 129
   Chapter 31 Define Your Offer 137
   Chapter 32 A Call To Action To Close the Sale 141
   Chapter 33 Why Track Your Ads? 143
   Chapter 34 How to Review Your Copywriting 147
   Chapter 35 Your Crash Course in Graphic Design 149
   Chapter 36 Your Company Logo 157
   Chapter 37 Graphic Design for Display Ads 163
   Chapter 38 Get Started With Online Advertising 171
   Chapter 39 Where Should I Advertise? 175
   Chapter 40 Set Your Advertising Budget 179
   Review of Part 3 181

Part 4: Stay Connected 185
   Introduction to Part 4 187
   Chapter 41 Serve Your Clients 189
   Chapter 42 Know Your Clients 191
   Chapter 43 Client Referral Systems 195
   Chapter 44 Lifetime Value of Clients 201
   Chapter 45 Reconnect With Past Clients 205
   Chapter 46 Your Website, Your Platform 209
   Chapter 47 Does Your Website Need a Makeover? 223
   Chapter 48 Create Your Marketing Planner 233

Chapter 49 Greeting Cards..237
Chapter 50 Emails Are Sales Letters...............................239
Chapter 51 Email Marketing...243
Chapter 52 Print Newsletters..247
Chapter 53 Client Letters Are Sales Letters....................251
Chapter 54 Client Appreciation Dinners 255
Chapter 55 Client Meetings Are Sales Meetings 259
Review of Part 4..263

Conclusion... 265

For Further Study.. 269

Index... 271

About the Author.. 275

Preface

Marketing Survival Guide is the first volume in the Local Business Success Series. In these books, I combine my experience as a marketing consultant, salesperson, chief financial officer, and small business owner to help business owners survive and thrive. Why start with marketing? Because your shortest path to higher sales and profits comes through better marketing of who you are and what you do.

This book teaches you how to think and act like a marketing consultant. You already know your clients and marketplace better than most marketing consultants. You can learn and apply proven marketing strategies in your business and see results quickly. You can do it yourself, save money, and stay in control.

I am an accidental brick-and-mortar business operator. In 2010, my marketing consulting company was retained by The Boardroom Executive Suites to revamp their marketing and advertising. The business needed my help because only a third of the offices were rented out. When the business changed hands six months later, the new owner asked me to manage everything. I agreed, and soon this client took over my life.

Now I can empathize with local business owners who struggle to grow their businesses while dealing with government regulations, taxes, accounting, staffing, and more in a very competitive and crowded marketplace.

Sound familiar? If so, then this book is for you.

My city of Grants Pass, Oregon, has about 35,000 people. Our chamber of commerce serves our city and county business community well. Since 2006, I've talked with hundreds of chamber members as a marketing consultant and as the operator of a local brick-and-mortar business. Many are stuck in a sales rut and need help. Sales are high enough to stay in business yet not high enough to be able to hire more help. Or take a vacation.

My unscientific survey tells me that 80% of my chamber of

commerce members cannot afford to pay my marketing consulting fees. Plus, I only have so much time, and I spend most of my time working on my own businesses these days. Without their money or my time, I could not help my chamber friends grow their businesses.

Now there is a way. I hope this book helps thousands of small business owners grow their businesses by being their own marketing consultant.

I also wrote this book to help my high school students from around the world. I teach the "Business II: Launch Your Business" course for the Ron Paul Curriculum. The course objective is to help students launch a business at 16 years old which will provide a middle-class income by their 21st birthday. With 180 video lessons, I teach them about the world of business and online business opportunities. My students develop valuable business skills such as website development, graphic design, copywriting, and publishing. Finally, each student plans and launches their first online business. You can learn more about this course at HighSchoolBiz.com.

Creating this high school business course forced me to break down business creation, marketing, and operations into simple steps. My students have limited time and money. My course takes one hour per day, five days per week, for the 36-week academic year. Students learn to make every minute count so that they can launch a successful business during high school.

Whether you are 15 years old or 50, by reading this book you can learn and implement proven marketing strategies to help your business survive and thrive now and in the years ahead. You can stop wasting your time on low-value tasks. You can stop wasting your money on ineffective ads. You can escape the rat race and really start enjoying your business and your life.

Richard Emmons
Grants Pass, Oregon

Introduction

Opportunity is missed by most people because it is
dressed in overalls and looks like work.

—Thomas Edison

Are you looking for a "million-dollar marketing secret" you can
implement today and have a line of customers outside your door
tomorrow? Sorry to disappoint you, but that isn't reality.

Marketing consultants do work for a living, so being your own
marketing consultant means doing marketing work. The good news is
that your competitors are likely too distracted or too lazy to invest the
focused and disciplined time needed to improve their marketing. You
can use proven marketing principles to double your sales without
spending more money on advertising.

Maybe you're asking yourself, "What is a marketing consultant?"

According to *The American Heritage Dictionary*, a consultant is
"One who gives expert or professional advice." A marketing
consultant is one who gives expert or professional advice in the area
of marketing. This advice includes market research, advertising,
pricing, and client communications.

Marketing consultants help business owners focus on the
marketing activities which provide the biggest long-term payoff in
sales and profits. This means focusing on marketing principles such
as market positioning and effective advertising. This also means
ignoring advertising fads which quickly flame out and stop working.
Being your own marketing consultant means thinking and acting like
a marketing consultant.

Marketing consultants do more or less hands-on work depending
on the size of the business. (And the size of the contract, of course.)

With my smaller business clients, I offer them my expert advice
and then implement my marketing strategies. I do all the work and
charge them accordingly. With larger clients, I do some of the work,

and they or a staff member do the rest. We act as a team.

In your business, you may be a one-person company, or you may be the boss with a bunch of worker bees cleaning carpets, baking pizzas, or mowing lawns. Yes, you'll need to do nearly everything yourself. You're the player-coach who needs to write the plays, run the plays, and handle offense and defense. When your company grows more profitable, you'll delegate or outsource some of the marketing and client work and take your business to an even higher level.

In medium-sized companies, you need to be the quarterback of the team. You call the plays which other marketing specialists run. Your marketing support team can include a graphic designer, marketing consultant, Google Ads specialist, a social media manager, website developer, and more.

In larger companies, you would be the team owner who wants to hire a talented coach, i.e., VP of Marketing, to lead the marketing effort. In this case, you need to know enough about marketing to hire the right person and keep their marketing efforts focused on growing your business, not on creating award-winning ads. You want to help your VP of Marketing hire the right team of players to move the company forward.

Whatever your situation, you can no longer afford to be like one of my past clients. His board of advisors told him to invest in marketing to grow his company. He ran a very successful construction company yet knew nothing about marketing. "I don't know what marketing is," he told me, "but I hear from others that you know, and I can trust you."

How much do you need to know about marketing? Consider this old joke:

> A bear jumps out of a bush and starts chasing two hikers. They both start running for their lives, but then one of them stops to put on his running shoes.
>
> His friend says, "What are you doing? You can't outrun a bear!"
>
> His friend replies, "I don't have to outrun the bear; I only have to outrun you!"

You don't need to become a world-class marketer to have a successful, fun, and satisfying business. You only need to out-market your biggest competitors. This book shows you how to do this.

Marketing Survival Guide walks you through a step-by-step process to upgrade your marketing and grow your business. Here's an overview of what's ahead.

In Part 1, we cover getting ready to grow your business. Do you feel swamped already? Join the club. Become more productive, and you'll free up time for marketing projects. You'll also free up time to handle an influx of new customers and clients.

In Part 2, you'll discover what makes your company unique and how to communicate this to your local area.

In Part 3, you'll learn how to create effective advertisements that get noticed by your target market and bring in new clients.

In Part 4, you'll learn how to stay in touch with your clients so they will come back to buy more, refer their friends, and never leave you for a competitor.

Finally, the book concludes with book recommendations to further your marketing studies. As a marketing consultant, you never know it all. As a business owner, you can never stop studying your market and applying effective marketing techniques. In *Marketing Survival Guide*, I boil down the most important and proven marketing strategies and tactics to help you grow your business quickly and sustainably. These other books guided me, and they can assist you as well.

How to approach this book

You'll encounter a lot of new information in this book. I know you're already super busy. I recommend this approach for learning and implementing the marketing strategies covered in this book:

1. Read the table of contents to get the roadmap of your journey ahead. Get your brain thinking about this. Know where you're heading.

2. Read this book quickly from beginning to end. Don't try to comprehend everything or implement anything. Write down ideas for your business and save them for later.

3. Don't skip the quotes which begin each chapter—a few by me and many by business and marketing greats of the past and present. These marketing golden nuggets will teach you something about

the chapter topic.

4. When you get to the chapter on building your client list, stop. Get a staff member to start this vital task while you work through the rest of this book. If you work alone, start gathering names and contact information while you read through the rest of the book.

5. Reread this book slowly a second time and complete the action steps. The book bonuses will help you implement what you learn into your business.

6. Yes, you should reread this book again later. You'll learn more each time because of your growing base of marketing knowledge, skills, and experience.

Now let's get started.

Part 1: Ready, Set, Grow

"...and you spent 6.35 years of your life
deleting spam from your e-mail."

Introduction to Part 1

You will never 'find' time for anything. If you want time,
you must make it.

—Charles Buxton

When you hire a marketing consultant, you invest money to buy time.
The marketing consultant spends his time working on your business.
Being your own marketing consultant requires freeing up some of
your time so that you can do it yourself. In many ways, you can do it
more quickly, because you know your target market and client base
better than an outside person.

You can't just spend more time on marketing alone. You need to
consider your sales process, your service delivery process, and the
administrative side of your business. These areas must become more
efficient because the goal of marketing is to get more new clients and
more repeat business.

Don't believe me?

If you doubled your business this week, could you double how
many hours you work? Probably not. Would you even want to? No
way. You need to learn how to work smarter now to avoid growing
pains later.

You also want to create consistent and proven marketing systems
for your business. These marketing systems take time, thought, and
energy to develop. Once in place, your marketing systems keep
working even when swamped with new clients.

All of this takes time, energy, and focus. We cover this in Part 1:

Chapter 1: Why You Want Clients, Not Customers

Chapter 2: How to Double Your Business

Chapter 3: Do "Marketing Magic Bullets" Exist?

Chapter 4: Your Marketing Mindset

Chapter 5: 80/20 Time Management

Chapter 6: Find More Time For Marketing

Chapter 7: Spend Less Time On Administration

Chapter 8: Spend Less Time On Operations

Chapter 9: Why Multitasking Destroys Productivity

Chapter 10: Five Ways To Work Smarter

Chapter 1

Why You Want Clients, Not Customers

> In a world that is trying to slam everyone down to commodity and marginalized status, you have to draw a line in the sand and distinguish yourself. And the way to do that is to start thinking of your relationship as an advisor, and the people you deal with as clients.
>
> —Jay Abraham

Let's begin with a close look at the word "clients." You may be a doctor, plumber, dry cleaner, lawyer, or insurance agent. You may have patients, customers, clients, members, or buyers. For the most part, I use "clients" in this book to refer to those people who buy products and services from you. Jay Abraham taught me why we should want "clients" rather than "customers" in our businesses.

Merriam-Webster defines a customer as "one that purchases a commodity or service." This sounds pretty bland to me.

The word "customer" comes from the same root word used for "customs" which you pay when returning from an overseas vacation with valuable items. The customs agent never expects to see you again. The same thing happens with large businesses like Walmart. They have millions of customers but don't have personal relationships with any of them. Big-box stores expect their customers to find the items they want and to self-checkout to make their purchases. Very impersonal. Very low prices and even slimmer profit margins.

Merriam-Webster defines the word "client" as "one that is under the protection of another, i.e., dependent" and "a person who engages the professional advice or services of another."

Attorneys don't have customers. Attorneys guide their clients to victory in court. And they charge healthy fees in the process.

Jay Abraham explains what "under your protection" means in his book, *Getting Everything You Can out of All You've Got*:

> In this case it means that you don't sell people a product or service just so you can make the largest one-time profit possible. You must understand and appreciate exactly what your clients need when they do business with you—even if they are unable to articulate that exact result themselves. Once you know what final outcome they need, you lead them to that outcome—you become a trusted adviser who protects them. And they have reason to remain your client for a lifetime.

When you treat your customers as clients, you won't need to chase prospects constantly. You'll get repeat business. You'll have clients for life. You'll spend less money on advertising. You will have escaped the rate race.

☐ **ACTION STEP: Start referring to your buyers as "clients" rather than "customers."**

Chapter 2

How To Double Your Business

> I have good news—there are only three ways to increase
> your business.
>
> —Jay Abraham

You must fix in your mind that you can and will double your sales by being your own marketing consultant. You begin this journey by understanding the mathematics of business growth. Your first lesson as a marketing consultant is knowing this formula.

Yes, there really are only three ways to grow a business. When you get small increases in these three areas, you get exponential growth in sales. I learned this from Jay Abraham over 25 years ago. Here are the three ways:

1. **Get more clients.** You attract more prospects and convert a higher percentage of prospects into clients.

2. **Increase your average sale.** McDonald's increased the sale of French fries 15% by merely asking, "Do you want fries with that?"

3. **Increase the frequency of repurchase.** You want your clients to buy from you more often. McDonald's added the Egg McMuffin and breakfast in 1972; by 1981 breakfast was 18% of sales. Now McDonald's serves breakfast all day long and sales are up even more.

These three sales growth factors work together to grow your company sales exponentially. Let's prove this by increasing each growth factor by 10%.

How much would this increase your annual sales?

When you increase these three growth factors by only 10%, your company sales increase by 33%.

	Current	Year 1
Clients (A)	100	110
Average Sale (B)	$100	$110
Purchases per year (C)	10	11
Annual Sales (A x B x C)	$100,000	$133,100
Sales Growth		33%

You want to double your sales in a year. Can you do this by adding more clients only?

Yes, you could do it this way. You would have to spend a ton of money on advertising to get enough new leads. Plus more time and money to convert them into new clients.

	Current	Year 1
Clients (A)	100	200
Average Sale (B)	$100	$100
Purchases per year (C)	10	10
Annual Sales (A x B x C)	$100,000	$200,000
Sales Growth		100%

Here's another and much easier way to double your business in one year. You increase the three growth factors by 26%. Not easy, but easier than doubling your number of clients.

	Current	Year 1
Clients (A)	100	126
Average Sale (B)	$100	$126
Purchases per year (C)	10	12.6
Annual Sales (A x B x C)	$100,000	$200,038
Sales Growth		100%

You can double your sales in two years with a 12.3% increase in the three factors. Two years may be more realistic for your business. Here's the calculation:

	Current	Year 1	Year 2
Clients (A)	100	112.3	126.1
Average Sale (B)	$100	$112	$126
Purchases per year (C)	10	11.2	12.6
Annual Sales (A x B x C)	$100,000	$141,625	$200,576
Sales Growth		42%	101%

You can double your business without increasing the number of clients. You do this by attracting better clients, and selling more to them more often.

For example, by increasing the average sale and repurchase rates by 40%, the company realizes a 96% increase in revenue.

	Current	Year 1
Clients (A)	100	100
Average Sale (B)	$100	$140
Purchases per year (C)	10	14
Annual Sales (A x B x C)	$100,000	$196,000
Sales Growth		96%

You nearly double your revenues serving the same number of clients. Your CPA will be blown away. You will be too.

Can I Really Double My Business?

Yes. Doubling your business seems like a daunting task until you break it down and work on these three areas in a consistent and effective way. By focusing on your marketing today, you'll reap big dividends in the years ahead.

You'll learn how to optimize your marketing in these three areas as you work your way through this book.

In Part 2, you'll create a unique selling proposition (USP) for your business. A strong USP sets you apart from your competition, positions you to attract more A-list clients, and helps you increase your average sale.

In Part 3, you'll learn how to get noticed by better, more qualified prospects. You'll learn how to structure effective advertisements, easy ways to improve your ads, and how to write using words that sell. You'll also learn ways to attract new clients without spending money on advertising.

In Part 4, you'll learn how to increase the frequency of repurchase by staying in touch with your clients. According to Bain & Company, it costs six times more to sell something to a new client than it does to an existing client. Staying in touch with your clients helps you in two significant ways. Your clients feel appreciated and not neglected. Your clients buy from you more often because they never forget how you can help them get what they want.

Does doubling your sales still sounds too good to be true? Please go back and reread this chapter.

ACTION STEP: Run the growth calculation for your business using estimates for the three growth factors. Re-run the numbers with a 10% increase in each factor. Imagine how you'll feel when you make this a reality. Be sure to download the book bonuses. You'll get an Excel worksheet to help you calculate how you'll double your sales. richardemmons.com/marketingbonus

Chapter 3

Do "Marketing Magic Bullets" Exist?

A "Magic Bullet" is something providing an effective
solution to a difficult or previously unsolvable problem.
—Webster's Dictionary

Every business owner has days like this: You wake up and tell yourself, "My business is stagnant, sales are flat, and the ads don't pull in leads like they used to. I have to get more clients. Today. How do I do it?" You want an unending supply of fresh leads so you can stop thinking about marketing. When you get to the office, you find the business card of the digital ad rep who came by last week. Should you call him up and say, "Let's do it"?

For most business owners, the answer should be "No." Why not? Because you'll waste time and money, and the effort will fail. You're looking for a quick, easy, permanent fix to getting more clients now and forever. These fixes don't exist.

I tell my prospects there are no marketing magic bullets because I don't want clients with unrealistic expectations. Do you?

- A financial advisor gets a new client whose portfolio just tanked 40%. The client wants to make back these losses in a year. Achieving this would require a 67% increase.

- A wedding coordinator lands a 33-year-old bride-to-be who wants a $10,000 Cinderella wedding in New York City for 400 guests in three months.

- A personal trainer gets a portly 50-year-old man who wants to run a marathon in three months to get over his mid-life crisis.

Do you see the common thread to these scenarios? Each client seeks a magic bullet to solve a problem that was years in the making.

- The advisor should tell the client to expect it to take three to five years to make up a 40% loss.

- The wedding coordinator should tell the fiancée to either delay the wedding, shrink the guest list, or have cake and champagne in her church fellowship hall.

- The personal trainer should start the guy with a 5K race this summer and wait until next year (or his next mid-life crisis) for the marathon.

What does this have to do with growing your business? You won't find marketing magic bullets which will quickly grow your business with little time or money. However, you will find marketing magic bullet salespeople. An ad rep can make bold promises in his quest to land a new account. How many advertisers guarantee results? Ever hear of a newspaper giving a refund on the classified ad when no one attends your open house? Me neither.

Magic bullet marketing activities can include:

- Running an untested full-page ad in a new glossy magazine.

- Paying a website developer to create a glitzy website.

- Spending money on Facebook ads because "everyone else is doing it." Ditto for Google AdWords.

Almost any unproven, untested marketing activity done in haste qualifies as a magic bullet marketing activity. Or anything requiring "just a few minutes of your time and your major credit card ... "

The moral to this story is that improving your marketing takes time and money. You can save time by hiring someone to help you get it done. Or you can invest your time and do it yourself when money is tight. That's the purpose of this book, because you can be your own marketing consultant.

Remember your own "magic bullet marketing" efforts of the past. Did you hit your target? Fire a blank? Or shoot yourself in the foot? I hope I shattered any illusions about finding a marketing magic bullet. Now let's get down to business.

☐ **ACTION STEP: Get over wasting money on fruitless marketing magic bullets in the past. That was then. This is now. Start reading Chapter 4.**

Chapter 4

Your Marketing Mindset

If you change the way you look at things, the things you look at change.

—Wayne Dyer

You run into an old buddy at your high school reunion. He asks the #1 icebreaker question, "So what do you do?" He expects an answer about your technical skills, which could be a financial planner, a wedding planner, or a funeral planner. Your answer focuses on how you want him to perceive you, which includes your education, experience, and what's on your business card. This is what you tell him.

What should you tell yourself? "I am a marketer." This means you see yourself as a marketer who focuses on defining, understanding, reaching, and serving your target market. As a business owner, marketing should be job #1 for you. This attitude affects how you view every aspect of your business.

- When a marketer meets someone new, he wonders how he might help that person reach his business and personal goals.

- When the phone rings, it's not a bother but rather an opportunity to speak with someone who discovered his website and wants to learn more.

- Every client interaction is an opportunity to earn (or lose) referrals.

- Marketing, like breathing, is done all the time. Not when the appointment book gets slim, or when sales stagnate.

- Hiring a new receptionist is a BIG deal for the marketer.

Let's take a closer look at this last bullet. If your company only gets one chance to make a good first impression, your receptionist will likely be the person to make it.

Will your clients care if your front-desk person knows the ins and outs of six major phone systems? Or types 100 words a minute? Or has a degree in business from your local state college?

Your clients won't know or notice any of this. However, they will notice your receptionist greeting them with a frown or a grunt. If your receptionist is "strictly business" or has to "turn on the charm" manually, you have a marketing problem.

Your receptionist ought to care enough about people to chit chat while your client waits. Perhaps offer some coffee, tea, or water upon their arrival. Ideally, your receptionist learns what your clients like to drink and gets it without asking.

This does several things for you. You learn more about your clients' lives and what's driving them that day. You gain a bit of slack if you're behind schedule and you can't start the meeting on time. People like doing business with people they like, and your receptionist has made YOU more likable.

Of course, knowing your phone system inside and out will help your receptionist better connect you to your clients. And typing 100 words per minute can help keep your files up to date. And a business degree might bring new ideas into your company and enhance customer service.

However, do these things really matter if your receptionist greets visitors with a frown for a split second before the smile kicks in? Or makes callers wish you had a direct dial number, so they don't need to "bother" the receptionist when they have a question?

Your marketing mindset helps you to hire the right person for every job, train them to know what's most important (treating people kindly and with respect), and the all-importance of supporting the marketing vision of your company. Of course, this goes for hiring everyone in your organization.

When you develop your marketing mindset, you'll view every aspect of your company from the eyes of your A-List clients. You'll suddenly see many areas to improve:

- Is your reception area clean and inviting? Or is it cluttered and awkward to navigate?

- What do your clients see as they walk from your reception area to your office or conference room? Files cascading out of dusty boxes, a kitchen with a sink full of dirty dishes, and a dark, dank restroom, or do they glimpse clean, tidy, inviting spaces?

- Does your desk make you appear disorganized, overwhelmed, and out of control, or productive and professional?

- Does your website look the same as it did five years ago ("This page is under construction"), or do clients or prospects have good reason to return frequently? Worse still, do you not have a website at all?

- Do your ads say too much about you, or do they showcase how your products and services help people?

- Do you use a Yahoo or Hotmail ("personal") account to correspond with clients, or does your email address reflect your business?

- Do you only speak with clients when they call you with a problem, or are you in touch and ready to move with them to the next level?

- Do you prioritize getting and serving clients, or are you socked in with administrative tasks like bookkeeping, which can be delegated or outsourced?

A marketing mindset, once developed, liberates you from the "administrivia" which drains time and energy and keeps you from growing your business and turning your clients into raving fans. At this very moment, you're reading a book about applying marketing principles and tactics to get more clients and sales. As Tony Robbins might say, you are unleashing the marketer within.

Now take a moment and imagine how you'll feel when your business stands out from competitors, your advertising is bringing in qualified leads, and your clients know you care about them and their success. Imagine a growing business without the uncertainty and stress of wondering how to compete in your marketplace, make payroll, or stop losing clients. When you imagine and remember this better future, you gain the edge you need to complete the tasks necessary to get it done.

Yes, your business card should say *Financial Advisor* or *Wedding Consultant* or *Personal Trainer*. Be sure to give one to your friend at your high school reunion. Remind yourself that your #1 job is to connect with, guide, and serve clients in your target market.

  ACTION STEP: Look in a mirror and say, "Marketing is my #1 job."

Chapter 5

80/20 Time Management

> Twenty percent of products usually account for about 80 percent of dollar sales value; so do 20 percent of customers. Twenty percent of customers or products usually also account for about 80 percent of an organization's profits.
> —Richard Koch, *The 80/20 Principle*

You need to read and apply this chapter in your business, or your efforts to double your business will fail or cost you a lot more work. Applying the 80/20 rule in your business gives you a massive advantage over your competitors. You significantly increase the probability of doubling your sales while reducing the day-to-day grind of running your business.

The 80/20 Principle was discovered by Italian economist Vilfredo Pareto in 1897. He calculated that 20% of Italy's population owned 80% of the land. This was true in every country he studied going as far back as he could find records. He also noticed 20% of the peapods in his garden contained 80% of the peas. While odd, the 80/20 rule has been observed all across society. For example, traffic studies show 20% of roads carry 80% of traffic. More importantly, the 80/20 rule applies to sales and profits.

Today, Apple has less than 20% of the global smartphone market yet enjoys over 80% of industry profits. In my primary business, I get 80% of my revenue from 20% of my clients. This means I get 20% of my revenue from 80% of my clients. Calculate this for your business. In this book, we assume that 20% of your clients generate 80% of your sales and profits. We'll refer to this group as your "20% Clients."

We'll refer to 80/20 again when you define your target market. For now, let's apply the 80/20 rule to time management.

In general, the 80/20 rule means 20% of inputs produce 80% of outputs. This means only 20% of your efforts result in 80% of your success. Conversely, 80% of your efforts result in only 20% of your success. You leverage your day by spending more time on 20% activities such as marketing and less time on 80% activities such as surfing the internet.

Here's how to get started today:

Stop your digital amusement for 30 days. Remove Facebook and Twitter from your smartphone. Let your spouse keep you current on the life and times of your friends and family. Do you use Facebook or Twitter for your business? Let someone else keep it current. You have better things to do. The same thing goes for Instagram, LinkedIn, Pinterest, and whatever newest/latest timewasting app is hot now.

Email is another time sink. How many e-newsletters clog your inbox every day? First, unsubscribe to any e-newsletters which you don't read the day they come in. You can always subscribe again later. Next, add rules or filters to automatically move other email updates to a folder for later review. Keep them out of your inbox so you won't be distracted. Get in, deal with clients and vendors, and then get out.

Stopping your social media feed and email inbox overload can add an hour to your workday. This reduces time spent on 80% activities to focus more time on 20% activities which grow your business.

80/20 Tip: You should help your employees focus more time on their 20% activities which produce 80% of their output. Eliminate their 80% time wasters, and you'll quickly improve their productivity on the job. You'll need this when your 20% activities result in more clients and sales.

You won't be overloaded with dozens of ways to grow your business in this book. You'll implement proven ways to grow your business by being unique, getting noticed, and staying connected. When you invest your time on marketing, you'll increase your sales and profits sustainably and predictably.

Next, we'll find more ways to create more time for marketing.

ACTION STEP: Remove Facebook and Twitter from your phone.

Chapter 6

Find More Time For Marketing

> The key is not to prioritize what's on your schedule, but to schedule your priorities.
>
> —Stephen Covey

You want to grow your business by increasing your focus on marketing. You know this will take time. However, you feel overloaded already. Where can you find some more time?

My daughter Victoria was getting ready for her high school graduation ceremony. Time was running short. She was getting stressed. Was it related to her hair or her outfit? I don't remember. I do remember Victoria crying out, "Time, time. I need more time!"

Don't you feel that way sometimes?

While you can't create more hours in the day, you can change how you spend your time each day. The first step is to see how you're spending your time now. Like every business, you spend your working hours in three main areas:

- Sales & Marketing to attract prospects and gain new clients;

- Operations to take care of clients with products and services;

- Administration, to include back-office work such as office management, accounting, and taxes. Finance lets you buy new equipment, spring for a company car, and make payroll.

I've spoken to many business owners and professionals over the years. The consensus is that "marketing is what I need to do, delivering services is what I like to do, and admin is what I hate to do but must do to get paid and stay out of trouble."

When time is tight, which area gets neglected? Sadly, marketing. Now take a look at your calendar and see how you spend your time in marketing, operations, and administration. Does your calendar only show time spent with prospects and clients?

In this case, you need to start tracking time spent on marketing and administration. You might be shocked at what you see. Or don't see. Too little time on marketing? Too much time on administration? Don't be discouraged. Your business may be doing okay now, when you spend only a couple of hours per week on marketing. Imagine what will happen when you spent 20% of your time on marketing.

Don't lump sales and marketing together. These are two separate functions, although you may do them both. What's the difference? Think of marketing as "leading the horse to water" and sales as "persuading him to drink."

Marketing is about attracting new prospects, as well as getting your existing clients to do more business with you. You do this with your website, printed and email newsletters, public seminars, display advertising, and all other ways of getting the word out about your business. This also includes making it easy for your clients to refer their friends and relatives.

Sales is persuading that prospect in your office, conference room, or showroom floor to place their trust in you and give you their business.

Sales and marketing activities work together to grow your practice. For example, a service professional without marketing materials, advertising, or a website has a much tougher job convincing the prospect in his office to become a client. Why? Targeted marketing efforts attract more qualified prospects while screening out others who aren't qualified. And marketing materials help tell your story well before your prospect walks in the door.

In the next chapter, we'll look at ways to spend less time on administration.

> **ACTION STEP:** Over the next five business days, track your time spent on marketing activities and your time spent making sales.

Chapter 7

Spend Less Time On Administration

You never want to be in a position where you can't make payroll.

—Brian Acton, co-founder of WhatsApp

When you want to free up time to spend on marketing activities, look first at administration. Finance and administration includes the back-office activities which support the sales and marketing and operations activities of your company. You have one or more employees; you need payroll. You have vendors; you need to pay the bills. You make a profit; you need to prepare tax returns. You have dust balls in the reception area; you need to vacuum. (What's that? You have a janitor or cleaning service for that already? Good for you.)

You need to delegate or outsource everything you can: a receptionist to answer calls, a bookkeeper to pay bills and invoice clients, a CPA to prepare taxes, a janitor to clean the office, and so on.

When I took over The Boardroom, I retained a local payroll service company to handle payroll. I simply email employee hours to my representative, Linda, and paychecks appear by courier the next day. The company handles all payroll tax reporting and payment of withholding taxes. Later I simplified payroll even more by shifting to monthly payroll from bi-weekly, thereby reducing 26 payroll periods to 12. This freed up time for marketing and operations.

You may or may not enjoy any of these administrative tasks. You may or may not have the education and experience to do them well. Spending more time on marketing means spending less time elsewhere. Especially administrative tasks.

I know one financial advisor who prepares his own personal and business income tax returns. He spends four hours every quarter for estimated taxes, two days in March for business returns, and two days in April for personal returns. This adds up to six days per year that are spent just on tax preparation—time that could be better spent advising clients or marketing his practice.

Consider this a rule of thumb: Outsource any task which can be done for less than your billable rate. If you bill out at $175 an hour, pay a CPA $100 per hour to prepare your tax returns.

Are you a one-person company without any staff? Do you need to do it all for now? Not necessarily. You just need to be more creative.

Consider locating your business in a professional business center like The Boardroom. Executive suites offer professional offices, a receptionist, conference rooms, and administrative services on an as-needed basis. You pay a monthly fee, which includes your office, telephone, fax, internet, janitorial services, and receptionist. You save time because someone else deals with these various administrative services. Many executive suites allow conference room and day-use office access in affiliated business centers. I helped an advisor in New Jersey who meets clients in various cities using a chain of business centers. His clients love the convenience of a nearby office. He saves money on office expenses. He boosts his brand by listing his various offices on his website. All without signing a long-term lease.

You could locate your office with a complementary business. For example, a financial advisor could locate her office with a CPA or attorney. The financial advisor gains the benefits of an executive suite, is available for referrals from the accountant or attorney, and gains visibility from their walk-in traffic.

Either option means avoiding the administrative details (and headaches) of running an office. You also add a receptionist between you and your clients. This makes your firm bigger than only you.

Finally, you can offload many secretarial, bookkeeping, and marketing tasks to a virtual assistant (VA). Hiring a VA gives you the productivity of a highly skilled administrative assistant without the cost, commitment and hassle of hiring a full-time employee.

Every minute cut from administration adds another minute to spend on marketing your business and taking care of clients.

☐ **ACTION STEP: Over the next five business days, track your time spent on administrative tasks.**

Chapter 8

Spend Less Time On Operations

Treat every day like it's the day before vacation, and you will get more work done!

—Zig Ziglar

In this chapter, we look at how to free up time for marketing by reducing time spent on operations. For service companies, operations includes client service development and delivery. For retail companies, operations refers to purchasing and retail store operations. For manufacturing companies, operations includes research and development (R&D) and manufacturing.

Becoming more efficient on the production side does two things for you:

1. You free up time to spend on marketing related activities.

2. You free up time to handle more clients.

Number two is critical because you (and your staff) must handle more clients in the same eight-hour day. Otherwise, getting more clients robs time from marketing activities. When you neglect marketing, your well runs dry, and you run out of prospects. Or you need to hire more staff, which means spending more time hiring and supervising.

Whether your business is established or just getting started, technology correctly used can quickly improve your operational efficiency. One hour saved per day means over 250 additional hours over a given year, time better spent getting and serving clients.

Some time ago, I had a client with decades of experience, excellent credentials, and happy clients in more than a dozen states. Yet he was a technology newbie to the extreme.

When I emailed him some questions, his assistant would print out the email for him. He would handwrite his comments and give it back to his assistant. She would fax it to my office. My assistant would call me to let me know I had a fax. When I was away from my office, I'd have her scan it in and email it to me. Incredible! Thankfully, he got a new computer and some training and soon replied to my emails via email. This freed up his assistant for more productive tasks.

At the other extreme, don't fall into the trap of adding technology just for technology's sake. A client once told me about his "Goldilocks" view of technology. Not too much technology, not too little, just the right amount. In this view, technology should:

1. Make you more money.

2. Save you time.

3. Provide information that helps your clients.

Operational activities serve current and future clients. "Production" takes care of current products and services. "Research and development" (R&D) looks ahead to develop future products and services. Knowing your market's wants and fears helps you innovate new products and services. Try to delegate current operations to other employees whenever possible. This frees you up to market current products and services and to create new products and services.

You should also give Zig Ziglar's tip a try.

This Thursday imagine that you're leaving on vacation Friday morning. You'll work like a madman tying up loose ends, cleaning out your inbox, and meeting with people to complete projects, while spending little or no time surfing the net or checking your Facebook feed. You might find you can devote all of Friday to being your own marketing consultant. If you can stay away from the office on your "vacation day" you can focus exclusively on marketing tasks and really get things done. Take enough of these marketing vacation days and soon you'll be able to plan and take a real vacation.

In the next two chapters, we'll look at ways to improve your operational efficiency without cutting service quality.

☐ **ACTION STEP: Over the next five business days, track your time spent on operations.**

Chapter 9

Why Multitasking Destroys Productivity

There is an illusion. The illusion is that technology, cell phones, email, faxes, text messaging, and whatever is latest-and-greatest all make us more productive. The reality, though, is that these things will only make us productive if we take control of them. They are the servants. We are the masters. If we do not protect our time, we will allow ourselves to be run over by the traffic of information.

—Dave Crenshaw

I begin this chapter with a lengthy quote from Dave Crenshaw's *The Myth of Multitasking: How 'Doing It All' Gets Nothing Done* because this book's premise is so important. Our brains can really only do one thing at a time. Instead, we do "switch-tasking" when we switch back and forth between two or more activities. Dave Crenshaw says switch-tasking tires the brain, thus lowering our overall productivity.

I fight this all the time when I'm at my computer; constantly checking email, Skype beeps for chats, and incoming calls from my receptionist. Each interruption distracts me and makes it harder to complete my important tasks.

You will make points with your clients by following one of my better habits. My cell phone is on silent mode 99% of the time and always this way during the business day. My clients appreciate it when my phone buzzes and I put the call into voicemail without looking to see who's calling me. Even when the client says, "Go ahead and take the call," I tell them, "I'm talking to you now," and they like that. They also learn I'll ignore their calls when I'm speaking with someone else. This applies "Do unto others as you would have them do unto you" to cell phone calls and texts. Maybe that's why they called it "manner mode" back in the 1980s when cell phones first came out. Think about it. Let's say I take the call from another client, prospect, vendor, or partner while I'm speaking to someone else in person. Either it's a problem, and I'll be thinking of a solution, or it's great news and I'll be thinking happy thoughts. Or it's simply a bother, and I'll be wondering why it couldn't wait.

Radios can be tuned to two different frequencies if they overlap slightly. You can hear two different songs or a song and a commercial. Tough to listen to. But possible.

Your brain can only tune into one conversation at a time. Either the person in front of you. Or the person calling you. Or texting you. Or instant messaging you. Just one.

Dave Crenshaw says "background tasking" won't hurt productivity. Some examples of background tasking include:

- Eating dessert while watching a video.

- Watching the news while doing three miles on the treadmill.

- Listening to a how-to podcast while driving.

This is common sense. You can walk and chew gum at the same time. You can run and chew gum at the same time. But you cannot walk and run at the same time. This activity is called jogging, and it's different. You can't chew gum and eat apple pie at the same time either. You have to choose.

Do the same thing when you're trying to get your most important tasks completed. Tune out everything you can, focus on the project in front of you, and stick with it until you get it done.

> **ACTION STEP 1: Give 100% attention to every person you are with today. This could be a client, a prospect, a friend, an employee, your spouse, or a child. Get ready to shock them.**

> **ACTION STEP 2: Give each task 100% attention until you get it DONE. Then move on to your next task. Tell your receptionist when you cannot be interrupted. Have her schedule callbacks with clients. You'll get more accomplished today. Now get to work.**

Chapter 10

Five Ways To Work Smarter

> Nothing is less productive than to make more efficient
> what should not be done at all.
> —Peter Drucker, *Managing for the Future*

You create more time for marketing activities by working smarter on everyday tasks. Two important tips on technology:

First, don't get caught up with technology because it's "cool" or fun. It must save you time, make you more efficient, or improve the quality of your products and services.

Second, you need to use cloud-based or multi-user versions of your software. You want your receptionist and other staff to do the input while you get easy access to up-to-date information. In today's world, the cloud is your friend, because your data is readily available to you and your staff from any computer or mobile device. Give this some thought even if you're currently a one-person company. Eventually, you'll hire an assistant, and you'll be glad you have multiuser software.

You can also get amazing apps for small one-time or monthly subscription fees rather than spending thousands to own the software or tens of thousands to hire a programmer to create custom software.

Here are five ways to work smarter and get more done in less time each day. Depending on your business, you may find these ideas incredibly helpful or laughably obvious. You may be "old school" or a hot young millennial. Either way, learning to work smarter each day frees up valuable time today and lays the groundwork for a larger business tomorrow.

1. Customer Relationship Management Software

Forget about using yellow sticky notes and 3x5 cards to track prospects. Referrals from clients and partners such as a CPA and attorneys are gold nuggets which can't be lost or forgotten. Instead, use customer relationship management software (CRM) to track your prospects and clients.

CRM software lets you set reminders when a prospect asks you to call them back in 30 days. You can put it out of your mind because the program will remind you in 30 days to call them back. You can quickly reference any notes you made from your previous conversation. This is especially helpful when you have a long sales cycle. Here are two CRM options to consider:

There are basic CRM capabilities built into QuickBooks Desktop. You can keep notes on each client plus send letters to particular clients based on specific criteria. QuickBooks Online doesn't include any CRM capability built-in yet offers several high-powered CRM apps which you can add to QBO for a monthly fee per user. This eliminates the need to enter clients into both QBO and your CRM. These cost between $12 and $49 per user per month.

Salesforce.com is now the #1 CRM software platform in the world. Their plans are $25 to $300 per month per user, which may seem like a lot when 3x5 cards are so cheap. However, you should compare the cost of any service to the benefit of eliminating paperwork and converting prospects to clients faster. CRM software helps you manage your clients, so nobody falls through the cracks. Forgotten prospects don't become clients; neglected clients often become former clients.

You should find a CRM solution which fits your business and your budget. You should ask around and get ideas from other business owners in your area. I also recommend going to PCMag.com. I've relied on PC Magazine reviews and recommendations for over 30 years. Yes, even back in the days when it was printed and had ads from hundreds of PC manufacturers. Search for "CRM" in the PCMag.com search box. You'll find lots of options to compare and consider.

2. Should You Go Paperless?

Yes, after you have your CRM software in place and enter all your clients. Then start scanning paper records and attach the PDF files to your client records. Eventually, you'll need less office space, your staff will be more productive, and you'll spend less time preparing for client meetings.

I know one advisor who went paperless from the beginning of his practice. He has instant access to all current and past client communications. He has a couple of file cabinets used mainly for payroll and accounts payable.

Being paperless takes discipline. Your assistant must scan in all documents as they arrive and attach them to your client records. Otherwise, you'll have piles of paper documents disconnected from your client files, and your CRM software will be incomplete or out of date.

I know another service professional who has a large room filled with file cabinets and tables covered with files waiting to be filed. His support staff spends many hours every day keeping track of the paperwork and getting everything filed correctly.

Naturally, newly established businesses have an advantage here. There are no file cabinets with decades of client records. Yet established companies gain the most from office automation because your support staff can become far more productive.

Depending on your situation, this may be an incredibly daunting task. Just get started. The longest journey begins with the first step. Over time you'll see major productivity gains. Convert your biggest clients first, and get to your smaller clients later. This is another application of 80/20 time management.

3. No More Fax Machine

You can eliminate a lot of paperwork by replacing your fax machine with an online fax service. One client has used the MetroFax service for many years. He and his staff love it. For under $20 per month, all his incoming faxes get sent via email to his receptionist's Outlook inbox. During the day, the receptionist routes the faxes to the recipients and attaches client-related faxes to the client contact record inside his CRM system. He kept his local fax number, so his business cards and letterhead didn't need to be reprinted.

His "faxes" now are emails with PDF attachments. You can do the same thing and dump your fax machine. Because your faxes are already digitized, your service assistant can forward important faxes to you wherever you happen to be. He or she would then attach them to the CRM client record for future reference.

You can also send outgoing faxes from within MetroFax. This client uses his main copier/printer/fax machine for outgoing faxes.

Eliminating paper faxes is an easy first step toward a paperless office and will save you time from day one.

4. Eliminate Handwritten Notes

One of my advisor clients was a painfully slow hunt-and-peck typist, and his handwriting was worse. Yet he is a very clear thinker and speaker. Let me share how he reduced his typing time by over 50%.

He used to take handwritten notes during client meetings and type them into his CRM program at the end of the day. When he was busy, his notes were less detailed and only hit the highlights. Sometimes the handwritten notes went into a folder with plans to type them in later. Often his assistant would ask him to decipher what he meant so she could get them entered into their CRM. While necessary, this process was tedious and always a pain in the neck.

No longer. He switched to the CopyTalk mobile scribe service. Immediately after each client meeting, he calls a phone number, then enters his cell phone number and a PIN. He has four minutes to describe what happened in the meeting:

1. What he learned about the client;

2. What he recommended to the client; and

3. What they will cover at the next meeting.

He hits the # key, and the system is ready for another message. Within two hours he gets an email with his spoken words typed (by a human being) as a Word document attachment. He attaches it to the client's record in his CRM application, and he is done. This saves him valuable time and allows him to provide better service to clients. His clients think he has a prodigious memory because he recalls so much detail from the previous meeting.

He uses this transcription service for more than client notes:

1. Client letter creation. He drafts client letters by calling CopyTalk and forwarding the email to his assistant. She copies

the message into the letterhead template and prints it for his signature.

2. Task delegation. Instead of verbally telling his assistant what he wants to be done, he delegates work with a detailed written description. He saves time, because he doesn't need to slow down and wait for her to scribble down some notes.

3. Radio scripts. He creates radio program scripts by practicing into CopyTalk. The printed "transcript" gives him something to reference in his own words.

My client noticed his staff was happier because CopyTalk eliminated a ton of tedious work and miscommunications. The staff now focuses on more productive tasks, such as helping clients and doing other marketing activities. You can learn more about CopyTalk services at copytalk.com. Financial professionals may qualify for a discount off the current monthly cost.

You can buy transcription software to avoid a monthly fee. The final quality will be lower because it is machine transcribed. You'll need to do some editing. Overall, it can save you a lot of time. Nuance Dragon ($300) has been the top program in this sector for over 20 years.

Like everything else, you need to weigh the benefit of these services against the cost. Don't buy it unless you plan to use it.

5. Use Your Smartphone To Work Smarter

Until Apple came out with the iPhone, I didn't realize I had a dumb phone. What makes a cell phone a smartphone? The ability to download and use apps, which are small applications made for smartphones. A smartphone is a handheld computer that makes phone calls.

The Pew Research Centers reports that 77% of Americans have a smartphone as of January 2017. This means that 23% of Americans do not. Are you in the 23%? Here are some reasons why you should get a smartphone now:

1. Android phones and iPhones offer built-in transcription as well as free and paid apps. Unlike CopyTalk, which uses human typists, the transcription is done by computer.

Humans do a better job now, but artificial intelligence (AI) makes the apps more accurate all the time.

2. Use your smartphone to stay on top of market conditions. One client used his smartphone to get stock market updates for his daily radio show. He found hot topic articles to discuss. No need to take his computer or print out articles.

3. Connect your phone to your calendar so you can set upcoming meetings with your client without having to interrupt your receptionist or write on a paper calendar.

4. You can stay caught up with your email when you're away from your desk.

5. Use your smartphone to take a picture of new clients, and add the picture of your client to his or her record in your CRM. This is a lifesaver when you have hundreds of clients and someone stops by the office to say, "Hello!"

I strongly recommend you get help with technology matters. Find someone who knows what's available and who can quickly implement solutions into your business. Otherwise, you'll spend hours researching technology options and many more hours implementing them in your business. You must focus on being your own marketing consultant. Let someone else be your technology guru.

ACTION STEP: Start working smarter by implementing one of these five ways in your business.

Review of Part 1

The relevant question is not simply what shall we do
tomorrow, but rather what shall we do today in order to
get ready for tomorrow.

—Peter Drucker

Part 1 can be boiled down to this: When you say "Yes" to being your
own marketing consultant, you must say "No" to other business
activities. This means eliminating unnecessary activities and
spending less time on less productive activities or delegating them to
someone else.

I'll summarize each chapter of Part 1 into a single sentence:

Chapter 1: Call and treat your buyers like clients for a lifetime
rather than customers for a day.

Chapter 2: You have only three ways to grow your business.

Chapter 3: Marketing magic bullets don't exist, so stop looking
for them.

Chapter 4: Developing your marketing mindset now leads to a
bigger, more profitable business later.

Chapter 5: 80/20 time management means you can achieve more
success while doing less work.

Chapter 6: Schedule time for marketing activities, or you won't
do them.

Chapter 7: Delegate or farm out administrative tasks better done
by a bookkeeper, payroll service, or CPA.

Chapter 8: Get more productive now so you and your staff can
handle more clients in the same eight-hour day later.

Chapter 9: Be focused, and you'll get more done in less time.

Chapter 10: Work smarter by wisely using technology in your
business.

Getting ready to grow never really ends. You should always look for ways to delegate tasks, simplify production and service delivery, and automate tasks to free up your time and that of your staff.

Now begin your journey of being your own marketing consultant.

Part 2: Be Unique

"If you are not 100% satisfied with your surgery,
the defective organ will be cheerfully refunded."

Introduction to Part 2

Be unique, or you'll be a commodity.

—Richard Emmons

Are you struggling to grow your business? Are your company's products and services viewed as commodities? Do you feel constant pressure to compete on price? Do you lose business to Amazon.com online and local big-box stores like Walmart? Are your advertisements no longer working? There is a way out. You will overcome your current situation by doing job #1 of a marketing consultant: clearly articulating your company's unique advantages to your clients and prospects.

You must define your uniqueness in your local market so people know why they should buy from you rather than from somebody else. Uncovering your uniqueness is the focus of Part 2 of this book.

You uncover and form your uniqueness by creating a unique selling proposition for your company. Never heard of "USP"? Neither have most of your smaller competitors. I say "smaller" because your larger competitors certainly have. You'll read some of their USPs in Chapter 13.

With a powerful USP, you maximize the results of all your current marketing efforts, including all your current advertising. You also raise the perceived value of your products and services, because you're no longer a commodity in your buyer's minds. In the produce market, organic fruits and vegetables sell for higher prices than "conventional" or commodity fruits and vegetables because of their real and perceived advantages. The same will be true of your products and services. Your USP should position you as the only viable solution for your industry in your local area.

What if you own a franchise? Hopefully, your franchisor is a marketing-savvy company with a powerful USP and a strong national brand. Or you might have a boring slogan which tells your customers nothing. In this case, you're stuck with it, because your franchise agreement probably prohibits you from changing the advertising. You should read your agreement carefully and see what you can and cannot do for local marketing.

As a franchisee, you can build up your personal brand within your community to make your business unique. In my city, the Pita Pit franchisee got involved in our local chamber of commerce. The husband-and-wife team volunteered in the community, donated food to good causes, and offered a chamber discount to chamber members. Together, they personalized the restaurant experience. We felt we were buying from them rather than a national company. Read this book with this example in mind, and see what you can do for your franchise. Who knows, maybe you'll suggest a winning USP and win Franchisee of the Year.

In Part 2, we'll build your brand with a powerful USP.

Chapter 11: Your Personal Brand

Chapter 12: Collect Testimonials

Chapter 13: What's a USP?

Chapter 14: Five Steps to a Winning USP

Chapter 15: Your Elevator Pitch

Chapter 16: Write a Biography That Sells

Chapter 17: USP Case Study: Financial Advisor

Chapter 18: USP Case Study: The Boardroom

Chapter 19: Putting Your USP To Work

Chapter 11

Your Personal Brand

Be yourself, everyone else is already taken.
—Gilbert Perreira

Peter Montoya begins his bestselling book, *The Personal Branding Phenomenon*, with these words:

> Define your brand or your brand will define you. Personal branding has always existed, but the key to success lies in taking control of this natural, inevitable process. (p. 13)

This chapter is about building your personal brand. I define personal branding as your reputation in your marketplace. The Cambridge Business Dictionary defines reputation as "the opinion that people have of someone or something, based on past behavior or character."

Your prospective clients can't view the future, but they can and will judge you on your past behavior and success. Interestingly, reputation and personal branding are far more important for CEOs and professionals.

We all know something about Sam Walton, Steve Jobs, and Walt Disney. They were founders and CEOs of small companies which became huge: Walmart, Apple, and Walt Disney Company. Do you know anything about the reputations of the senior vice presidents of these companies?

Sam's Club and Walmart were named after Sam Walton. Can you name a Walmart CEO from the past 20 years? Me neither.

When you go to Disneyland, are you interested in the personal branding of individual cast members who sell the tickets, run the rides, or dress up as Mickey Mouse? Nope.

Few people had heard of Apple Chief Operating Officer Tim Cook or designer Jonny Ive until Steve Jobs was diagnosed with cancer.

Suddenly their business reputations mattered a lot, so Apple brought them out from beneath the shadow of Steve Jobs.

If you are a financial advisor, lawyer, architect, insurance agent, or salesperson, your reputation in the marketplace will make you or break you. People are trusting you with their hard-earned money, so your reputation matters a lot. Company reputation is equally important for retailers and manufacturers.

In today's socially networked world, you can't separate "personal" from "business." Would you hire an employee with a wild reputation on Facebook? No? Then why would you expect someone to hire you if you have a wild reputation online? Assess every post, update, photo, video, or tweet on how it helps or hurts your professional reputation.

Great marketing cannot overcome defective products or horrible customer service. Same thing is true with reputation. Building your reputation in the marketplace leads to referrals, repeat business, and long-term client retention.

Gary North teaches the "Business I: Introduction to Business" course for the Ron Paul Curriculum. He teaches students how to build a reputation for reliability over time and almost guarantee their success in life:

1. Do what you say you are going to do.

2. Do it at the price you agreed on (or a little lower).

3. Complete your work on time (or a little early).

These three success habits are easy to understand yet tough to do all the time. Falling a bit short in this area? As my mom used to say, "It's never too late to start doing the right thing." Get started today.

> **ACTION STEP: Write down these affirmations on paper. Say them out loud. Begin doing them. Make them your habits.**
>
> **1. I do what I say I will do.**
>
> **2. I do it at the agreed-upon price.**
>
> **3. I complete projects on time.**

Chapter 12

Collect Testimonials

Let someone else praise you, and not your own mouth;
A stranger, and not your own lips.

—King Solomon, Proverbs 27:2

You will be creating your USP in the following three chapters. As you complete this process, you will hear amazing testimonials about your business and its products and services. Pay close attention during this step, and you'll capture powerful testimonials. These golden nuggets will turbocharge your marketing efforts by giving you credibility with prospects and reminding clients why you're the best.

80/20 Tip: Your best testimonials come from your best clients. These are the people you help the most. You want more of these clients because they are in your top 20% client group. When you use these testimonials in your advertising, you will connect with prospects similar to these 20% Clients.

What if your industry doesn't allow testimonials in your advertising? This is true for lawyers, financial advisors, and health practitioners. In this case, you should collect testimonials and use them to build case studies. I learned this workaround from marketing strategist Sean D'Souza. Case studies should include technical jargon a reader would expect to find in a technical white paper or case study.

You can get powerful testimonials from prospects who didn't buy from you. "I never felt pressured to buy or guilty when I decided not to go forward."

You can get powerful testimonials from your vendors. "They are easy to work with, and they always pay on time if not early."

You can get testimonials from your employees. "They value my feedback and listen to my ideas."

Local community leaders give testimonials which carry extra weight in your community.

Make a regular practice of obtaining testimonials from your clients. How do you get great testimonials? As they say, "If you don't ask, you don't get." You must ask for testimonials. Get over any awkwardness, because testimonials are marketing gold.

Video testimonials are the most believable, because they are the hardest to fake or enhance during the editing process. When you hold a seminar for your clients, set up a video camera so you can ask attendees to give video testimonials during breaks. Do you have a retail business? Set up a camera and ask people to say positive things about your business.

You can also ask for testimonials via email. Be sure to prompt your clients to help them articulate what you want to hear. Many movies follow the hero's journey storyline. You can elicit similar "hero's journey" testimonials from your clients by asking three questions:

What was your situation before you did business with us?

How did we help you?

What is your situation now?

Sometimes a client will say something about how you helped them. You should immediately say, "Can I quote you on that?" In most cases, he or she will say, "Of course." Don't ask them to send it to you in writing because few will do it. Instead, write it down and send it to them in an email. Ask them to confirm what they said, and thank them for letting you use it in your marketing efforts. In this way, you are making it easy for them to give you the testimonial you want to receive.

It's not bragging when someone else says it. Testimonials provide proof that you deliver what you promise you will do. Capture these words today, and you will capture more business in the future.

☐ **ACTION STEP 1: Start a new document named Testimonials. Collect testimonials from every source you can think of. Enter the date and context of the testimonial. Edit for brevity.**

☐ **ACTION STEP 2: Go to Amazon.com and leave a 5-star review for this book. See how easy it is to ask?**

Chapter 13

What's a USP?

A USP is the hidden secret of literally thousands of the most successful advertising campaigns ever written.
—Rosser Reeves, *Reality in Advertising*

"USP" stands for "unique selling proposition." The unique selling proposition is also called the sustainable service advantage or extra value proposition. Copywriter and direct marketing expert Dan Kennedy defines USP this way:

When you set out to attract a new, prospective customer to your business for the first time, there is one paramount question you must answer:

"Why should I choose your business/product/service versus any/every other competitive option available to me?"

Your prospects have three choices: buy from you, buy from a competitor, or do it themselves.

- For financial advisors, wealthy people can do business with you, another advisor, or manage their money themselves.

- For dry cleaners, people can get their dress shirts dry cleaned by you, have them done by another dry cleaner, or iron them at home.

- For steakhouses, hungry people can buy a steak dinner from you, eat one at another restaurant, or grill it on their home BBQ.

- For doctors, sick people can see you, find another doctor, or research online and buy some herbs and vitamins.

Prospects must be given a reason to do business with you rather than their current service provider or doing it themselves. You must remind your clients that doing business with you remains their best choice. Your USP will do that for your business.

Rosser Reeves invented the term "USP" in the 1960s. In *Reality in Advertising* (1961) he defines what makes a good USP:

1. Each advertisement must make a proposition to the consumer. Not just words, not just product puffery, not just show-window advertising. Each advertisement must say to each reader: "Buy this product, and you will get this specific benefit."

2. The proposition must be one that the competition either cannot, or does not, offer. It must be unique—either a uniqueness of the brand or a claim not otherwise made in that particular field of advertising.

3. The proposition must be so strong that it can move the mass millions, i.e., pull over new customers to your product.

Here are some well-known examples which meet this three-part definition:

Domino's Pizza: "You get fresh, hot pizza delivered to your door in 30 minutes or less—or it's free." Notice it says nothing about Mama's recipe, taste, or low price. Their USP created a whole new market at a time when it took 30 to 40 minutes to get a pizza at pizza restaurants.

Federal Express: "When it absolutely, positively has to be there overnight." This USP answered the question, "Why would anyone in their right mind pay FedEx ten bucks to mail a letter?"

M&M's: "The milk chocolate melts in your mouth, not in your hand." Rosser Reeves created this USP over 40 years ago, and it still works well.

Wonder Bread: "Helps build strong bodies 12 ways." Maybe it does, maybe it doesn't. This USP sold a lot of bread because it differentiated Wonder Bread from all other white bread.

Did it occur to you that three of these USPs are no longer used by their companies? What they use now doesn't qualify as a USP by Rosser Reeves' definition.

Wonder Bread now uses "It's soft, white and as wholesome as childhood itself." They also use "Spread the wonder," which may be a subtle reference to peanut butter and jelly sandwiches.

Federal Express does a lot more today than parcels and overnight delivery. Now they have retail stores, overnight, freight, and logistics services. FedEx's current brand slogan is "What We Deliver By Delivering."

The Domino's Pizza website doesn't currently have a slogan or a USP. You can help a charitable cause and earn points toward free pizza. Only Domino's knows if this works or not. I read this guarantee in the "Legal Stuff" fine print on Domino's home page:

> Our Guarantee: If you are not completely satisfied with your Domino's Pizza experience, we will make it right or refund your money.

This guarantee should be highlighted on Domino's website. Not buried where 99% of web visitors won't see it. A great guarantee helped take Domino's Pizza to number one. Don't hide what makes you unique.

Here are some other well-known USPs:

- Walmart offers price leadership: "Save More. Live Better."

- Target promises higher quality: "Expect More. Pay Less."

- Home Depot serves DIYs: "More saving. More doing."

- McDonald's: "Quality, Service, Cleanliness, and Value"

- United Airlines: "Fly the Friendly Skies of United"

- Google: "To organize and deliver all information to everyone."

What Makes Amazon.com Unique?

In 1995, Amazon.com advertised itself as "Earth's biggest bookstore." That was back then. Now Amazon offers just about everything. How Amazon does business can be described with one word: Easy.

- Amazon makes it easy to buy things. One-click easy.

- Amazon makes it easy to read product and book reviews.

- Amazon makes it easy to read books with Kindle.

- Amazon makes it easy for authors to publish books.

- Amazon makes it easy to ask buyers about products.
- Amazon makes it easy to store files in the cloud.
- Amazon makes it easy to return things
- Amazon makes it easy to become an Amazon vendor.
- Amazon makes it easy to rent and watch videos.
- Amazon Prime makes it easy to get free shipping.

Amazon also makes it easy for local brick-and-mortar retailers to lose sleep at night. Is there a way to compete with Amazon?

Yes. Local retailers can compete effectively with Amazon by providing a personal and customized buying experience. Employees at one ladies' boutique in my area text pictures of new purses and outfits to customers as a "first look" advantage. A reply text will hold the item for three hours. Many retailers can offer free delivery and installation. You should always work on making it easier for clients to do business with you.

Why should a powerful USP be the foundation of your marketing program? Without a USP your advertising will have a generic, "plain vanilla" appearance which doesn't grab attention or lead people to act. With a compelling and memorable USP deployed in your advertising, you'll attract more 20% Clients. A good USP can also repel folks who aren't your targeted clientele.

Now you need to create a USP for your business. The next chapter shows you a five-step process to do this. Be sure to read the rest of Part 2 before you begin this very important task.

ACTION STEP: Reread this chapter right now. USPs are really that important.

Chapter 14

Five Steps To a Winning USP

> The possibilities for building a USP are unlimited. It's best, however, to adopt a USP that dynamically addresses an obvious void in the marketplace that you can honestly fill.
>
> —Jay Abraham

This chapter is the most important and most demanding chapter of this book. As a marketing consultant, I know creating a strong USP is the first and most important step in the marketing makeover process. Everything else follows from a strong USP. With a strong USP, my business and my clients' businesses stand out from the crowd. Ads generate more leads and sales. Clients return to buy again and again. A strong USP will do the same for your business.

I learned how to create unique selling propositions by studying and practicing the work of marketing greats such as Jay Abraham, Dan Kennedy, Richard Johnson, and Bill Bodri. Now I'm going to teach you how to create a USP for your business.

You will follow a five-step process to create your company's USP.

Step 1: Examine your (the owner's) perspective

Step 2: Talk to your employees

Step 3: Interview your best clients

Step 4: Compile interview answers

Step 5: Formulate your USP

You'll learn a lot about your company as you go through the USP creation process. You'll put on your interviewer's hat and ask a few very important questions of partners, clients, and employees. Marketing expert and master interviewer Michael Senoff says, "I am not afraid to ask hard questions." He gets great answers this way, and so will you. You won't like every answer. Get over it! A complaint introduces another way to improve your business and makes it easier to do business with you. Now let's get started on your company's USP.

Step 1: Examine your (the owner's) perspective

As the owner of the business, you need to ask yourself what makes your company unique.

What do we do which makes our company great?

How does what we do well benefit our target market?

Why do we think our clients buy from us? Try your best to be objective.

What have our clients said in the past about our products and services?

There are lots of ways to be unique. Of course, your uniqueness must benefit your clients. Here are 20 ways to be unique:

1. Education (advanced degrees and certifications)
2. Experience (more years doing it)
3. Personality (people like doing business with you)
4. Price (better price; lowest price is tough to maintain)
5. Terms (easier to understand and more ways to pay)
6. Stress-free sales process (no-haggle pricing for buying cars)
7. Product selection (do you own a niche?)
8. Product quality (greatness)
9. Product delivery (faster or cheaper)
10. Service selection (do you own a niche?)
11. Service quality (greatness)
12. Service delivery (better client experience)
13. Pain relief (do something people hate to do themselves)
14. Quality of life (you make life better in a major way)

15. Guarantee (Is it better than your industry standard?)

16. Convenience (more locations or better hours)

17. Easier website shopping experience (Amazon or website cart)

18. Association (endorsed and used by a well-known person)

19. Emotion (how it makes people feel when they own it)

20. Exclusivity (no one else can offer it in your city)

Your unique benefit to your target audience will be in one or more of these areas. Write out every benefit you can think of. You may come up with benefits that only you know about.

If you have multiple owners and senior managers in your company, then have each person assess the company's uniqueness. This should be done individually and then as a group.

Step 2: Talk to your employees

You want to get your employees' perspective. You can send a survey to your employees. You could hold one or more roundtable discussions.

Ask them the same questions you used in Step 1. Keep asking follow-up questions to dig deeper and get complete answers.

Unless someone objects, audio record your USP research sessions with employees, vendors, and clients. You want to keep the conversation flowing yet be able to go back later and get their exact words.

What do we do which makes our company great?

How does what we do well benefit our target market?

Why do you think our clients buy from us? Try your best to be objective.

What have our clients told you in the past about our products and services?

You may want to have someone else facilitate this discussion. Don't attend if you want to encourage an open discussion—or if you get offended easily.

Don't be surprised if your employees don't know what makes your company unique. You'll train them later on your USP as you integrate it into your business operations. For now, get their ideas and write them all down.

You may also be surprised at some very insightful answers. Remember, your employees are on the front lines dealing with clients every day. They hear the complaints and the compliments. Listen to them. Learn from them.

Step 3: Interview your best clients

In this step, you or an associate will conduct telephone interviews with 20 to 50 of your top clients. These clients really appreciate you, your company, and how you do business. You want to learn, from their perspective, what makes you different. You will ask them a series of questions and any follow-up questions to dig deeper and gain a better understanding of your clients' thinking.

As you talk to your best clients, listen carefully to their answers and take detailed notes. Dig deeper when they say something you weren't expecting. Don't evaluate or judge anything they say. Don't get defensive! Do you feel embarrassed or are too busy to call them yourself? Then have someone else call up and ask the questions. You need to get these answers.

Here are the four questions as directed to a CPA firm. You should adapt these questions to your own business.

1. *"Why did you initially start doing business with ABC Accounting?"*

When you ask clients why they initially bought from you, you can uncover a hidden USP for your business. What first got their attention? Was it your advertising? Which ad? Or a referral from another client? Online?

2. *"Why do you continue to do business with ABC Accounting?"*

You want to find out what keeps your clients from going elsewhere.

3. *"Have you ever used another CPA? What did you like or dislike about that CPA compared to us?"*

You want to learn ways to improve your business and stop losing clients to competitors.

The answers to questions one to three reveal golden nuggets. You'll use them as testimonials in your marketing materials. Your prospects will read them and say to themselves, "Wow! I wish my advisor/lawyer/plumber was that way with me." You also learn why folks prefer you over other similar companies. You want specific examples like:

- "He always explains my options until I understand them. He never makes me feel stupid."

- "I can always get hold of him ... even when the market's tanking."

- "You let me express my concerns and kept quiet until I got it all out!"

4. "Is there anything we can help you with now?"

This final question brings the conversation to a close. You might reveal additional products or services to sell them now. You can also get ideas for future products and services. Both help you increase the lifetime value of your clients.

Step 4: Compile interview answers

At this point in the process, you've gotten answers from yourself, your partners, your employees, and your top 20–50 clients. If you recorded your interviews and focus groups, you need to get them transcribed. Get all this data in front of you. Read it several times to help you spot trends and valuable golden nuggets. Search for everything unique about you and your business. Why did your best clients start doing business with you? What attracted them? Why *you* over anyone else?

List all the benefits mentioned by your partners, clients, and employees. Look for significant benefits that no else offers in your marketplace. You should ask "So what?" to every benefit, because it may not matter to your clients.

You need to study your competitors and potential competitors to discover their USPs. You should set aside any benefit which your competitors offer. Don't be a copycat. If it's not unique, you need to keep digging. You can look for USP ideas from similar businesses in other cities or even other industries.

You'll have some great testimonials, so be sure to save them to use later on your website and in other marketing materials.

Step 5: Formulate your USP

Keep your USP concise, easy to say, and easy to remember. This approach makes it easy on you and your employees to tell others about it. It also makes it easier to include it in an advertisement.

Your USP should identify your target market. Don't try to appeal to everyone. FedEx originally targeted people who absolutely needed it delivered overnight. This FedEx USP also targeted a void in the marketplace which only it could fulfill. I remember when the Postmaster General of the US Postal Service used FedEx to send an important document. He embarrassed the post office and delivered fantastic publicity to FedEx.

Keep it relevant. Does it matter to your target market? If your USP is not relevant to your target market, no one will care, and it won't help you grow your business.

Keep it compelling so your targeted prospects will hear it and take action. Don't settle for a USP which makes hearers ask, "So what?"

When someone hears it, will it generate conversation? When every other pizza restaurant took 45 minutes to make and bake a pizza, people wondered how Domino's could guarantee 30-minute delivery. You need a big promise ... yet not so big it's not believable. Your staff must deliver on this promise.

Don't get hung up in the writing process. Write out numerous USPs, and mix and match your words. Sometimes USPs came quickly to me, but mostly I'd write out dozens of combinations to find the winner. Get help with this step from someone who can write well.

Think you have a winner? Then compare your USP to those of your competitors. Is your USP really unique? Can it be easily copied? Try to make it both unique and difficult to copy. Domino's Pizza delivered on their USP with special pizza ovens and a fast delivery system. This took years for competitors to copy.

Here's another lesson from Domino's Pizza. They created their USP on what they wanted to become, not what they had done in the past when they only had a few restaurants. You can define uniqueness for your company with your USP and then grow into it.

For example, you set your company apart with a new and unusual guarantee. Your existing clients benefit by your new and higher standard of performance. Prospects now give you a look because your bold guarantee sets you apart.

Finally, never forget you are a unique individual, and your company is unique. The "U" in "USP" stands for "unique." Be yourself. Don't be bland. Stand out from your competitors.

> **ACTION STEP: Create your USP. Be sure to download the book bonuses. You'll get worksheets to help you research and create your company's USP.** richardemmons.com/marketingbonus

Chapter 15

Your Elevator Pitch

> Why does it matter how you answer the question "What
> do you do?" when speaking to someone you don't know?
> Because you never know when the person you're
> speaking to turns out to be a potential customer or
> referral source.
>
> —Bob Bly, *The Marketing Plan Handbook*

Now you will expand your USP into an elevator pitch. Your elevator
pitch answers the question, "So what do you do?" in 30 to 60 seconds.
You get this question from people who have no idea what you do, such
as someone in an elevator. You have his attention for a moment. You
want to quickly and memorably describe how you help people.

The wrong way to answer is "I'm a financial planner." Or saying,
"I am a carpet cleaner." You'd get points for brevity yet make zero
headway toward turning them into a prospect or getting a referral.
"That's nice" would be a typical response.

A-List Copywriter Bob Bly popularized sales trainer Paul Karasik's
three-part formula for devising a successful elevator pitch. In his book
The Marketing Plan Handbook, Bob explains the concept using a
female financial planner:

> What is the formula? The first part is to ask a question beginning
> with the words 'Do you know?' The question identifies the pain or
> need that your product or service addresses. For a financial
> planner who, say, works mostly with middle-aged women who
> are separated, divorced, or widowed and possibly re-entering the
> workplace, this question might be, 'Do you know how, when
> women get divorced or re-enter the workforce after many years
> of depending on a spouse, they are overwhelmed by all the
> financial decisions they have to make?'

The second part of the formula is a statement that begins with the

57

words 'What I do' or 'What we do,' followed by a clear description of the service you deliver. Continuing with our financial planner, she might say, 'What we do is help women gain control of their finances and achieve their personal financial and investment goals.'

The third part of the formula presents a big benefit and begins 'So that.' Here's what the whole thing sounds like: 'Do you know how when women get divorced or re-enter the workforce after many years of depending on a spouse, they are overwhelmed by all the financial decisions they have to make? What we do is help women gain control of their finances and achieve their personal financial and investment goals so that they can stay in the houses they have lived in all their adult lives, have enough income to enjoy a comfortable lifestyle, and be free of money worries.'

You may be asking yourself, "Sounds great, but would it get approved by my compliance department?" Good question. Maybe that's why it's called the elevator pitch, so no one else hears you say it. Of course, you may need to get it approved if your advertising is regulated.

This elevator pitch formula is:

"Do you know ... ?"

"What I do is ... " or "What we do is ... "

" ... so that ... "

Once you've written your elevator pitch, commit it to memory and practice saying it in front of a mirror. If you stumble and bumble your way through it, your listener won't be impressed. You must practice this until you can nail it every time.

You'll find this helpful at networking meetings, because you can summarize what you do and who you help in under a minute.

Maybe you work in a two-story building. Here's a formula for a very concise elevator pitch: "I help [target market] by doing [major benefit]." Example: "I help divorced and widowed women live financially secure and independent lives."

☐ ACTION STEP: Write your elevator pitch. Practice it in front of a mirror.

Chapter 16

Write a Biography That Sells

> Bob Bly is a freelance copywriter and marketing consultant with 3 decades of experience in business-to-business and direct response marketing.
>
> —Bob Bly, bly.com

In Chapter 14, we created your USP or "unique selling proposition." Your USP sets you apart from your competitors and reminds your clients why they do business with you. Unfortunately, a USP for financial advisors and other highly regulated professionals can be very constrained.

Why? Financial advisors cannot use a pithy 17-word USP screaming a big benefit for clients, because compliance departments won't allow it. Imagine if M&M-Mars had a compliance department:

> M&M's chocolates may melt in your mouth not in your hands; however, past performance is not an indicator of future outcomes. The performance of a single M&M may vary substantially from the composite performance of all M&M's in the bag.

Ouch. Painful to read and definitely not worth spending hundreds of millions of dollars in advertising over the years.

You create the best USP you can within the confines of your industry. When you can't make a big promise in your USP, you do the next best thing. You write a biography that sells. This is your story told with a purpose.

You start with all the biographical details you gathered during the creation of your USP. Your education. Your experience. Why you became a lawyer/advisor/realtor. Your travels. Your hobbies. Your family. Think of interesting and unique events in your life.

All of these facts are woven together to tell your story in such a way as to build confidence, chemistry, and credibility. Your past helped form you into the financial advisor you are today. You can also weave in information about your staff's education and experience to highlight the uniqueness of your team. Tell your story in a way to attract more A-list clients.

I interviewed one advisor who offhandedly mentioned he'd once bowled a 300 game. I spun that fact into the following bio:

> "No bowler averages 300. You want someone who has experience and a track record of consistent high performance ... Steve held a 200+ bowling average for over 20 years. And he did roll a 300-game and has the ring to prove it!"

Notice I didn't say that this advisor provides consistently high financial performance. I talked about his bowling hobby. Because lots of retired people enjoy bowling, the story connected this advisor with his clients and prospects. When I wrote about avoiding "financial gutter balls" they knew what I was talking about. You'll read his USP and biography in the next chapter.

This story illustrates another important point. You never want your story to be boring or abstract. You want to be personal and engaging, which means talking about yourself, your family, and even your employees.

You can use these stories during sales meetings. If you target golfers at your country club, talk about your first round of golf, your greatest triumph on the green, and your most embarrassing round. Think these little details are trivial? I spoke with a financial advisor who was a boating fanatic. I told the story of how I capsized my little boat on my first solo sail. He got a good laugh, and I got a new client.

Remember that your story is just a means to an end. Your clients may find it interesting, but it must implicitly answer the question, "Should I do business with this person?" You must answer this crucial question. Remember, you want prospects to trust you with their money. Your story must support the idea that doing business with you is a wise move on their part—regardless of your bowling average.

> **ACTION STEP:** Write your personal biography or company history as a soft sales pitch for your products and services. You'll post this on the About page of your website. Looking for ideas? Read the next two chapters and then do it.

Chapter 17

USP Case Study: Financial Advisor

Finally, Plain English Answers to Your Retirement
Questions.

—Richard Emmons

I did a lot of work for financial planner Steve Kirkendall back in 2008 including a USP, biography, and website. He generously let me include it in this book as a case study. Steve has refreshed his website twice since 2008, yet the copy remains the same because it continues to reflect who he is and what makes him unique.

Financial advisors are closely regulated by state and federal agencies including the Securities and Exchange Commission. This includes marketing activities, including all advertising. Financial advisors cannot make promises, use client testimonials, or offer performance guarantees.

This reality made my job much more challenging. I asked Steve lots of questions about his practice, education, experience, and what he did for fun. He liked what I came up with. I hope you can learn from it and come up with something you can use for many years as well.

Unique Selling Proposition

Steve's USP addresses two common concerns of retired and soon-to-be retired people: They hate jargon, and they want to be heard.

Finally, Plain English Answers to Your Retirement Questions

On the next page you'll see how this appeared on his website.

Kirkendall Financial Services
"Finally, Plain English Answers to Your Retirement Questions"

A generous man will prosper; he who refreshes others will himself be refreshed.
Proverbs 11:25

Now you will read four articles I wrote for Steve's website.

Website Home Page

Ever talk to someone who retired too soon and worries about running out of money? Or worries about how to transfer their assets to their children rather than Uncle Sam?

Stephen R. Kirkendall, ChFC, is a Chartered Financial Consultant with nearly 30 years' experience. KPDQ-FM radio host Lew Davies invited Steve to his Liveline show for over 15 years. Why? Because Steve would take every call, take it seriously, and answer the caller's question in plain English.

Steve has also previously given over 100 educational seminars at colleges and churches. His television interviews have been seen by national audiences.

Steve has helped hundreds of individuals and couples assess their financial situation and risk tolerance, determined their retirement goals, and helped them create a plan to pursue their retirement goals. He has helped many widows understand their investments after the loss of their husbands and cope with their new responsibilities and situation.

An avid bowler, Steve can help you avoid the many "gutter balls" of retirement strategies. Some people save too little or take too little risk. Others take too much risk and lose money they don't have time to earn again. Still others retire too soon and risk running out of money during the latter years of retirement.

Don't lose sleep over retirement because you don't know where you stand. Let Steve help by determining your current situation, developing a strategy, and reviewing it with you to help keep you on track. Maybe then you can enjoy your time with the grandkids.

Do you really want to feel in control of your financial future? Give Steve a call today!

A Biography That Sells

A Story of Serving Others

The son of a soldier, Steve was born in Portland, Oregon, and raised in a military family which lived across the United States and in Europe.

Steve first worked in a commissary helping military wives load groceries. Working for tips alone, he learned to work with people and saw the rewards of being paid for performance.

After attending five different high schools in Germany and America, Steve became the first person in his family to graduate from high school. This experience helped him to get to know people and make friends. He also learned how to communicate in plain English to be understood in a foreign land. Today, his clients appreciate plain English explanations of complex financial investments, what's going on in the economy, and how to help them meet their retirement goals.

After graduating from high school, Steve returned to Portland to settle and find employment. His first job was as a doorman in a theater. While he enjoyed meeting new people and directing them to the best seats, it was mostly saying hello and goodbye. He also found himself in his first "wage job" earning less than he did as a 12-year-old loading groceries. He often asked himself, "How can I really help other people and make a good enough living to support my family?

Steve began his career in the financial services industry when he began doing mobile home, home equity, and student loans at Equitable Savings and Loan. He helped many families during this time of the Savings and Loan meltdown as Equitable Savings was absorbed by Benj. Franklin Savings in 1982 which later became a part of Bank of America in 1990. While the logo on his business card changed, Steve never wavered from his commitment to provide his clients with unvarnished facts about the economy.

He loved the opportunity to help people fulfill their dreams of homeownership and a college education. In time, Steve became the first loan officer in the Portland area to put on educational seminars for real estate agents.

He taught realtors how to do their own qualifying VA/FHA loans and save their homebuyers money.

After eight years of helping his clients buy homes, finance college dreams, and insuring life's risks, Steve wanted to help his clients with all phases of their financial lives. This led him to become a full-service financial planner with Royal Alliance in 1984. Ever the student, Steve became one of Oregon's first Certified Financial Planning practitioners when he earned his CFP(R) designation in 1986.

In 1987, Steve began offering "Successful Money Management" seminars in colleges and in churches. He has given well over 100 seminars in the past 20 years as he sought to educate the public on financial matters and let folks get to know him better.

Steve soon had the opportunity to reach thousands of people at once on KPDQ-FM. Talk radio host Lew Davies asked him to answer listeners' questions on all sorts of financial matters. Steve's deep and wide experience in financial matters and his time-tested ability to speak in plain English made him a popular guest for over 20 years.

This radio opportunity and many public seminars allowed Steve to help more and more people with their retirement planning as time went by.

Steve remained self-employed as a representative for a couple of securities companies as he built his financial planning practice. Unfortunately, as time went by, each company would pressure him to sell company products which provided higher commissions to the company. When he didn't sell them, he didn't seem to get the attention he needed to help his people. They also wanted him to charge more for his advice.

Steve realized that he needed the freedom of being an independent financial planner to best pursue his clients' needs. He gained this ability in 2000 when he founded his own company, Kirkendall Financial Services, and aligned with a securities company that didn't push their company product. No longer would he be told how to do things by people who didn't share his philosophy.

Steve's service to his clients has spanned six presidents. He has seen high inflation, sky high interest rates, recessions, stock market booms and busts, savings and loan crises, and terrible mortgage products which hurt homeowners and banks alike. Steve feels blessed to use his education and experience to treat his clients as he wishes to be treated.

Steve lives in Vancouver with his wife and enjoys playing, hiking, and reading with his five young grandchildren.

Avoiding Gutterballs

Why bowling is like planning for your retirement

An avid bowler, Steve can help you avoid the many "gutter balls" of planning for your retirement.

Some people save too little or take too little risk to get the returns they need. Others take on too much risk, so money is lost when they're too old to earn it again. Others retire too soon and risk running out of money during the latter years of retirement.

Steve often tells his clients that "working just one or two more years can add as much as 10 years of retirement income on the backend. Better to know you'll be short at 80 years NOW and work a couple more years than find out when you're 80 and it's too late."

No bowler averages 300. You want someone who has experience and a track record of consistent high performance ... Steve held a 200+ bowling average for over 20 years. And he did roll a 300-game and has the ring to prove it!

So whether you are planning your retirement or bowling with some friends on a Saturday afternoon, keep the ball rolling down the middle of the lane and avoid those gutter balls!

Steve Kirkendall On KPDQ Radio For 15 Years

During the 15 years he was on Lew Davies' Liveline radio show, Steve became an institution on the radio in Portland. Why?

Steve would take eight to 20 callers per one-hour show. He took all incoming calls and took them all seriously. He could encapsulate what the issue was, outline several different ways to approach it, and explain everything in terms the caller could understand. He'd let them take it from there. He never said "buy this stock" or "put this much in this area," because Steve won't give financial advice without a full understanding of the caller's personal situation.

Liveline was an audience-driven show where the callers drove the agenda. Steve never knew where the calls were coming from. Many planners would never subject themselves to this type of program, because they might get a question they couldn't answer. Steve took every call which came in.

Thankfully, in 15 years of taking calls, Steve never received a call from a disgruntled client who could have vented their frustrations to 30 to 40 thousand people!

I want you to learn from these examples as you create your own USP and company story. If you're a financial advisor, please don't use this copy as your own. Make your USP and message uniquely yours. Otherwise, you risk throwing a marketing gutter ball, and that would be embarrassing.

☐ **ACTION STEP: Review your own story for ways to make it better.**

Chapter 18

USP Case Study: The Boardroom

Be more professional, productive, and profitable with
your office in The Boardroom.

—Richard Emmons

In this chapter, we look at the unique selling propositions I created for
The Boardroom Executive Suites. The Boardroom offers full-time,
part-time, and virtual offices to business professionals in Grants Pass,
Oregon.

The Boardroom began as a marketing and public relations client.
I handled the grand opening and initial marketing of The Boardroom
and The Guild Building in 2007. After The Boardroom opened, I
moved my marketing consultancy from my home office to an office in
The Boardroom. I handled sales whenever someone came by to look
at available offices.

In early 2010, The Boardroom hired me to handle all of their
marketing activities. I created a USP, marketing flyers, and a website.

Later that year, the ownership of the building and The Boardroom
changed hands. The new owner wanted to be the landlord only and
not manage the operations of The Boardroom. The previous manager
and receptionist had recently left The Boardroom. The new owner
asked me to take on the management of The Boardroom on a strictly
pay-for-performance basis. I agreed and expected this to be a part-
time gig. Not exactly.

In the beginning, "pay for performance" meant 60-hour weeks
and zero pay. I revamped The Boardroom's operations, sales and
marketing, and administration. I began earning money as The
Boardroom filled up with new Boardroom Members. Starting out with
a 32% occupancy rate, we're now consistently 90% to 100% filled.
Many thanks to my hardworking staff.

Now this brick-and-mortar business client takes between 20% and 80% of my time. I spend the rest of my time on other projects, such as writing books.

My early work on the marketing and sales really paid off when I took over the management of The Boardroom. I was far too busy overseeing the staff and tackling all the administrative functions to do any marketing brainstorming. Finding time for marketing can be very difficult at times, especially when I need to recruit, hire, and train a new employee.

Invest time now a give yourself the gift of marketing. You'll realize when you need it most that marketing is the gift which keeps on giving: landing new clients and keeping your existing clients buying more.

I feel the pain of all the brick-and-mortar business owners out there. I get it that it's tough to find time for marketing. However, do the work now, and you'll reap the rewards now and in the years ahead.

Enough time down memory lane. Now back to the study of USPs.

My original USP served The Boardroom well for over six years.

"Be more professional, productive, and profitable with your office in The Boardroom"

I combined The Boardroom's unique office services with something you don't usually get with office space. I'm referring to ...

A Money-Back Guarantee

This risk reversal is typical in most industries. In the commercial real estate market, it's unheard of—that is, until I added it to The Boardroom in 2010. A guarantee adds to the uniqueness of The Boardroom and speaks of our confidence in delivering on the promise of the USP.

"30 Day 100% Money Back Guarantee!"

If during the first 30 days you're not totally satisfied with your Full-Time Office services for whatever reason at all, simply let us know and we'll cheerfully refund 100% of your money.

You can be innovative in your industry when you borrow a standard marketing practice from another industry.

I put this USP to work in brochures, flyers, radio ads, and TV ads on local cable stations. Our marketing challenge was to educate the market on what "executive suites" meant and get them to come in for a tour. We got the word out and got lots of foot traffic. The USP worked very well.

Time for a New USP

There is a common thread to everything we do at The Boardroom. We make it easy for a business professional to have a great office in Grants Pass, Oregon. We handle all the back-office work, including telephone answering, managing vendors, internet, stocking the kitchen, conference rooms, and janitorial. All delivered in a professional office environment.

Most companies delegate these tasks to a CFO (chief financial officer) or an Office Manager. One-person companies let the owner do this all themselves. (This is why I recommended executive suites back in Chapter 7.)

It all gets back to making it easy to have a professional office. We've used this slogan on some of our marketing inside The Boardroom.

"We make doing business easy."

This slogan makes "easy" explicit to the reader. We use this headline with images of The Boardroom and copy bullets on what's available. However, it begins with "We" which violates what I cover in Chapter 25. In short, "we" focuses on what we do rather than focusing on what the prospect needs. Plus, it's not unique and too vague for a USP. I like it, but we can do better.

"Get a Great Office in Grants Pass. Today."

This USP is short and sweet and implies "easy" because it solves the problem for any business professional needing a nice office right now. Maybe she lost her lease. Maybe he wants to open a satellite office in Grants Pass. Perhaps someone wants to escape the isolation of a home office. Plus, professionals want a great office because their office is a reflection of their professionalism.

This hypothetical USP echoes FedEx's original USP:

"When You Absolutely, Positively Need a Great Office in Grants Pass. Visit The Boardroom."

I won't use that as our USP, but it will make an attention-getting headline for an ad in our local chamber of commerce newsletter.

A "great office" can be a part-time office rather than a full-time office. There are tons of people working out of home offices. Where do they go when they need to meet a hot prospect, a coffeehouse? No way. I've been there and done that, before The Boardroom. Be my own receptionist? No, I did that before The Boardroom opened and had distracting, annoying and occasionally awkward interruptions.

Website Home Page

On the website, I put this new USP into the subhead beneath the main headline. The main headline provides the solution to a business professional's problem: He or she needs a professional office now or very soon.

Here is the new USP for The Boardroom as seen on our website:

"Get a Great Office in Grants Pass. Today."

How to Be More Professional, Productive, and Profitable

With your office in The Boardroom, you'll be more professional in every aspect of your business. Your calls will be answered by a receptionist and not by you on your cell phone. Your clients will appreciate the easy, off-street parking away from the bustle of downtown. You'll hold your important meetings in one of The Boardroom's fully-equipped conference rooms.

You'll also be more **productive** because you'll have a quiet office to get your important work done. You won't get distracted by cold-calling vendors. You get great technology without having to deal with the phone company, the internet service provider or any of the hassles of leasing commercial office space.

Finally, you'll be more **profitable** because you can focus on marketing and client services rather than back office complexities. You enjoy the benefits of a professional office space while sharing the expense with over 30 other business professionals. You won't sign a lease or need to commit to multiple offices when you only need one. As your business grows, you can add another office when you need it (subject to availability.)

Source: https://www.theboardroomsuites.com/ (retrieved 1/5/2019)

This headline makes two big claims. First, the office will be great.

The subhead provides three major benefits to back up this claim. Second, the person can get an office today. This can't happen with commercial office space. Negotiating and signing a commercial lease, utilities need to be ordered and installed, a phone system needs to be installed and set up, and so on. All of this can take weeks. It may be great (eventually), but it isn't fast, and it isn't easy.

☐ **ACTION STEP: Review your USP and look for ways to make it better.**

Chapter 19

Putting Your USP To Work

> You and your employees must live, breathe, and act your
> USP at all times.
>
> —Jay Abraham

You have discovered and described your company's uniqueness in your USP. Now you can tell your past, present, and future clients about what makes you unique and why it matters to them. You'll do this by putting your USP to work in your advertising and whenever you communicate with your clients.

As an example, let's modify Walmart's current USP, "Save money. Live better." into a concise, powerful, yet never-to-be-approved-by-compliance USP for a fictional financial advisor.

"Make money. Retire sooner."

Where could you put this USP to work? You can start with these:

1. Your website banners. Change your header graphic, and every page of your website will be updated.

2. Your website About Us page needs to emphasize what makes you different. Elsewhere you would give examples of how you make this USP a reality for your clients.

3. Your client statements. You can put your USP in the footer or the cover page of the statement.

4. Your sales proposals. You want your USP to appear near your picture or logo so it won't be missed.

5. Your answering machine message: "Thank you for calling John Smith & Associates, where we help you make money and retire sooner. Please leave us a message."

6. Your email signature block.

7. Your fax cover sheet.

8. Add it to your byline in articles you write.

9. Add it to introductions when you speak in public.

10. Your 30-second announcement at chamber of commerce events.

11. Your newspaper and magazine advertisements.

12. Your press releases.

Some places may need to wait until you need to reprint:

1. Your business cards.

2. Your printed brochures.

3. Your letterhead. Consider adding your USP to the bottom of your signature block until you reprint your letterhead.

4. Your checks. You never know if one of your vendors needs a financial advisor and wants to retire sooner.

5. Your yellow page ads, if you still have one.

6. Your billboards. Unlikely, I know, but what about the sign on the front of your office?

7. Your employee training manual.

The last one seems odd at first glance, but it's critical when integrating your USP into your operations.

Imagine one of your employees being asked, "What makes your boss different from all the other financial advisors out there?" What would she say? Imagine a Federal Express employee being asked in 1978, "Why should I pay ten bucks to mail a letter?" "I don't know" would be the wrong answer.

Your employees should know exactly what makes you different and be able to explain why you're the best option. You must deliver on your marketing promises, so your employees must be trained to deliver on your USP. Proverbs 29:18 states, "Where there is no vision, the people perish." When you teach your employees about your USP, you give your employees a vision of why your company is the best choice for your clients and similar prospects.

I received an example of this in an email from a ZipRecruiter.com hiring specialist. He weaves in Ziprecruiter's USP, which at the time was, "We deliver a quality candidate to 80% of employers within a single day."

> I wanted to follow up to let you know we now deliver a quality candidate to 80% of employers within a single day. We're extremely proud of the work we're doing around here and would love to prove it to you when you have your next hiring need.

Here's an example from over forty years ago. My mom found a letter written to me on April 23, 1976. I had written M&M-Mars after getting some red, green, or brown coloring on my hands while eating some M&M's. I can't remember what motivated me to write this letter. Maybe it was a school assignment. Maybe I was just being a wise guy.

Here's how M&M's replied:

Dear Richard:

Thank you for your letter and your interest in M&M's Chocolate Candies.

In our advertisements we say: "THE MILK CHOCOLATE MELTS IN YOUR MOUTH—NOT IN YOUR HAND". The melting to which you referred was undoubtedly caused when the pure food coloring in the thin sugar shell came in contact with the moisture in your hands. This sometimes happens if the candy is held for a while.

The objective of our advertising is to acquaint consumers with the fact that M&M's Chocolate Candies are neat to eat and do not have the mess of other chocolate products that do not have thin sugar shells protecting the chocolate centers.

Thank you again for your interest in writing to us.

Very truly yours,

(Miss) Eleanor C. Trautwein

Customer Service Manager

Among other things, Miss Trautwein's reply showed that M&M's understood the importance of having employees know their USP.

Your USP connects all of your advertising and client communications into a cohesive whole. Get the word out, and you'll attract prospects who want and appreciate what makes you different and better. You'll build a brand based on your USP so no one can copy you without being "me too."

□ **ACTION STEP: Write down 10 ways to get the word out about your USP.**

Review of Part 2

> Don't be intimidated by what you don't know. That can
> be your greatest strength and ensure that you do things
> differently from everyone else.
>
> —Sara Blakely, founder of Spanx

You'll get 80% of the value of this book by creating a USP for your business and letting your prospects, clients, employees, and vendors know about it. Being unique in your marketplace is that important.

Of course, there are better and worse ways of getting your message out to your marketplace. No self-respecting marketing consultant would create your USP and then go on to the next client. He would also fix your advertisements so you get more sales bang for your advertising buck. That's what you'll learn how to do in Part 3 of this book.

Will you ever need to refine or replace your USP? Pitching legend Satchel Paige said famously, "Don't look back. Something might be gaining on you." That may be true in baseball, but not in business. You must keep your eyes fixed on the marketplace. This includes your clients, prospects, and competitors.

In 1875, Montgomery Ward had a powerful USP in "Satisfaction Guaranteed or Your Money Back." This powerful USP took away the risk of buying by mail order. Sears copied it in 1887. Now money-back guarantees are the norm in business. Both companies were later overrun by "smaller" competitors because they lost their edge. First, by Walmart on the retail level and then online by Amazon.

The best way to keep your USP unique is being the first one known for it in your marketplace. Anyone after you will be seen as "me too" if they attempt to copy you. You maintain your reputation by delivering on your marketing promises. You also do it through your advertising campaigns.

A powerful USP can serve your company for ten or more years. That gives you a massive return on investment for your time.

I'll summarize each chapter of Part 2 into a single sentence:

Chapter 11: Your personal brand reflects your reputation in the marketplace.

Chapter 12: Seek, obtain, and use testimonials about your business.

Chapter 13: Your USP tells prospects why they should buy from you rather than a competitor or trying to do it themselves.

Chapter 14: Create a winning USP in five thought-provoking steps.

Chapter 15: Your elevator speech can turn strangers into prospects.

Chapter 16: Your personal or company story builds trust and leads to sales.

Chapter 17: Case study 1: The USP and personal story of a financial advisor.

Chapter 18: Case study 2: The USP and a brief history of The Boardroom Executive Suites.

Chapter 19: Put your USP to work and leverage your marketing efforts.

Your next lesson as a marketing consultant is to learn how to create effective advertisements. You'll use your USP and proven copywriting techniques to maximize the marketing return on investment from your current advertising.

Part 3: Get Noticed

©Glasbergen
glasbergen.com

GLASBERGEN

"Never mind what your mother told you.
In advertising, it's OK to brag!"

Introduction to Part 3

> If you don't get noticed, you don't have anything. You
> just have to be noticed, but the art is in getting noticed
> naturally, without screaming or without tricks.
>
> —Leo Burnett

In Part 1, you freed up time to focus on marketing now and handle more business later. In Part 2, you invested some of that time to create a USP for your business. You defined who you are, who you want to serve, and what sets you apart from your competitors. Now it's time to start getting noticed by your targeted prospects. You'll do this with better ads.

It would take entire books to teach you how to become a professional marketing consultant, copywriter, or graphic designer serving dozens of businesses in dozens of industries. That's okay, that's not your goal. You just need to learn what you need to know to improve the advertising of your business in your industry. That's what this section of this book is all about. As a bonus, you'll also know enough to intelligently oversee the work of professional marketers, copywriters, and graphic designers later.

This section begins with a chapter on how to get noticed without advertising. You may find this especially helpful if you have more time than money now.

In Chapter 21, you learn how to get new clients using endorsement letters. **You may find endorsement letters to be the single most powerful client acquisition technique taught in this book.** Yes, I bolded that sentence so you can't miss it.

Effective advertising gets you noticed by your targeted prospects and sells them products and services.

Chapter 20: Get Noticed Without Advertising

Chapter 21: Get Clients with Endorsement Letters

Chapter 22: Effective Advertising

Chapter 23: Image Advertising

Chapter 24: Direct Response Advertising

We spend the next 13 chapters learning how to create better ads. This includes the words (or copy) used in ads as well as graphic design basics. You won't become an advertising pro, but you will know numerous ways to improve your ads with better copywriting (words) and graphic design (layout). By improving your ads, you attract the people you want as clients and repel the people you can't help or would prefer not to help.

As a marketing consultant, you start by improving what is currently working. Later you create new ad campaigns on new advertising platforms.

Chapter 25: The Easiest Way to Fix Your Ads

Chapter 26: Creating Effective Ad Campaigns

Chapter 27: Know Your Market and Define Your Avatar

Chapter 28: Seven Copywriting Basics

Chapter 29: Successful Advertising Formulas

Chapter 30: Grab Attention with Your Headline

Chapter 31: Define Your Offer

Chapter 32: A Call to Action to Close the Sale

Chapter 33: Why Track Your Ads?

Chapter 34: How to Review Your Copywriting

Chapter 35: Your Crash Course in Graphic Design

Chapter 36: Your Company Logo

Chapter 37: Graphic Design for Display Ads

Finally, we take a look at online advertising, where you should advertise your business, and how much to spend on advertising.

Chapter 38: Get Started With Online Advertising

Chapter 39: Where Should I Advertise?

Chapter 40: Setting Your Advertising Budget

Chapter 20

Get Noticed Without Advertising

Networking is marketing. Marketing yourself, marketing your uniqueness, marketing what you stand for.
—Christine Comaford-Lynch, *Rules for Renegades*

You can get noticed by prospects without spending any money on advertisements. When you have little or no money for advertising, you have to get creative and invest your time. Otherwise, no one will know you exist, and your business will die a slow death.

Let's talk about networking. Networking does not mean hanging out with random groups of people and talking about the weather. You must network with a purpose. In his book *Endless Referrals*, Bob Burg says, "Networking is the cultivating of mutually beneficial, give-and-take, win-win relationships."

Let's take a closer look at his definition. A farmer knows he has to plant seeds to cultivate a crop. Nothing grows overnight except (it seems) weeds. I watch business owners show up to a networking group, hand out business cards to everyone present, and then never show up again. Those business cards might be used as a bookmark, but they won't be used to make referrals. That's a win-lose attitude and a proven recipe for failure.

Chamber of Commerce

Joining your local chamber of commerce gives you the most networking bang for your marketing buck. This tactic is especially helpful for very small companies with very small marketing budgets.

In my city, a small business can join the chamber for $250 per year. The chamber provides many opportunities to network with hundreds of other business owners. Every Wednesday morning, we have a "Business for Breakfast" meeting where chamber members get

30 seconds to update everyone on what's happening in their life, both business and personal. Every week you get to tell 60-80 business owners and salespeople who you are and what you do. You can sign up to host a meeting for the price of coffee and some Costco muffins. Do it at your business location, if you have room, or host it at your local library, Grange, or business center.

Chamber members also attend chamber educational and social events. Many chamber members only buy business services from other chamber members. This could be you. My chamber is always looking for members to volunteer on various committees. Our Chamber Ambassadors go to ribbon-cutting ceremonies, chamber events and help out in many other ways. Being a Chamber Ambassador costs you time but not money. Twice I've emceed my chamber's annual awards banquet. I have lots of fun doing it and get better known by hundreds of people in attendance.

Other Networking Opportunities

You can also get involved in other business networking groups. Business Networking International (BNI) has groups in many cities. There are lots of other independent networking groups out there. You can look at Meetup.com to find other groups which meet in your area.

I highly recommend joining a Toastmasters club. You'll improve your communication and leadership skills while getting to know other highly motivated people in your local community. I helped start a Toastmasters club in 2012 as a spin-off of a business networking group. You learn to deliver prepared speeches, think on your feet for impromptu speeches, and how to be a better listener—all helpful skills to make you a better networker. Toastmaster dues are now just $45 every six months. Locate clubs in your area at Toastmasters.org. Visit a few clubs and find one which fits your schedule and personality.

Networking groups give you the opportunity to get referrals as well as give referrals to other competent business professionals. As Jay Abraham says, "No one ever succeeds without the help of others." Networking helps you succeed and have fun at the same time.

You can also help out a local nonprofit in your community. I have served on the board of directors of my local Gospel Rescue Mission for 18 years. In this position I have worked with church leaders, a radio station owner, local government officials, and numerous other business leaders. Yes, this takes time, but it's well worth it when I see so many responsible homeless people transition back into community life.

Getting Noticed Grab Bag

You have many, many other ways to get noticed without spending money on advertising. Some are easy and take little time. Others take a lot of time and effort.

- You can write articles for your local newspaper. You'll position yourself as an expert and become a local celebrity of sorts.

- You can barter your products and services for free advertising.

- You can throw your business cards up in the air when the bride and groom leave their wedding.

- You can post flyers on community bulletin boards where your buyers buy other things.

- You can tell 10 friends about your business and ask them to tell 10 of their friends about your business. Suddenly 100 more people know about your business.

- You can post pictures of your products on Pinterest.

- You can offer a complimentary service to support local nonprofit events.

- You can use press releases to get mentioned in your local newspapers, TV, and radio shows.

- You can be a guest on a local radio show.

- You can write a book. (In the old days, a familiar warning was "Don't try this at home!" In this case, I warn you, "Don't try this at the office!")

All of these activities will help you build your personal brand and get your company noticed in the community.

☐ **ACTION STEP: Join your local chamber of commerce.**

Chapter 21

Get Clients With Endorsement Letters

> You can get everything in life you want if you just help
> enough other people get what they want.
>
> —Zig Ziglar

Endorsement letters help you get great clients quickly for not much
more than the cost of postage, letterhead, and an envelope. You may
be able to double your business using this one idea alone. Yes,
endorsement letters are that powerful.

Ask yourself, "Who else helps people who are my ideal clients?" I
am not talking about your competitors. I am talking about
complementary, non-competitive companies who are well-respected
in your city. Think of businesses with clients you would love to have
as your clients.

For example, you know an insurance agent who specializes in
helping small businesses. You could be a CPA, financial advisor, or
lawyer who could help this same type of client. You write a letter which
gets printed on the insurance agent's letterhead. He offers something
of value to his clients that you would provide. Here's an example of a
Christmas letter from an insurance agent to his clients:

Dear John,

It's hard to believe it's December already, and Christmas is just
ahead. I could send you a calendar or day planner, but you would
probably toss it out because you use a smartphone now.

Instead, my gift to you is something which could save you
thousands of dollars in the years ahead.

Sally Johnson, CPA, has helped small business owners like you
save serious money on their taxes for many years. She has
creative but safe strategies which save money and reduce audit
risk for business owners like you. You may benefit from using

similar strategies.

Sally has already helped some of my clients who raved to me about her service. Now she can help you save money on your tax bill.

I have arranged for you to get a second opinion on your last year's business and personal tax returns. Sally will review your tax returns and then meet with you to discuss her ideas on how you can save money on your taxes. There is no cost or obligation to you, of course. I hope you'll save money on your taxes, so you'll have more capital to grow your business.

You won't be bugged if you're not interested. Just call Sally's office at 555-444-3333 and mention this letter. You'll get one of the time slots for a full one-hour consultation.

Please let me know how this works out for you. And one more thing ...

Merry Christmas!

My best,

Bill Evans
Insurance Agent

In this letter, Bill has endorsed Sally to his clients. He transferred some of his goodwill to Sally. Bill's clients trust Sally more because they already trust Bill. This endorsement letter will be far more effective than Sally sending cold letters, postcards, or emails to a rented mailing list.

To paraphrase Zig Ziglar, Sally will get what she wants out of life when she helps Bill's clients get what they want in life. In this case, a lower tax bill.

Sally pays to print the letters and apply a real postage stamp to each envelope. Bill signs the letters with a blue pen and mails them to his clients. Sally can print and send a thousand letters for a couple thousand dollars. Every 1% conversion rate means ten new clients for Sally. Let's assume each new client pays Sally $1,000 for personal and business tax returns. Ten new clients would generate $10,000 in recurring revenue on a $2,000 mailing.

That's a five-to-one marketing return on investment in year one only. The lifetime value of these new clients will be enormous.

A client endorsement "Christmas Letter" can be done every year.

Of course, Sally can send a similar endorsement letter promoting Bill to her clients. By integrating Bill's USP into the letter, Sally's clients would be intrigued by how Bill's unique service could benefit them.

Here are some other complementary endorsement letter opportunities:

- Accountant and estate planning attorney
- Pizza restaurant and ice cream parlor
- Clothing store and dry cleaner
- Paint store and flooring store
- Financial planner and insurance agent
- Real estate agent and pool supply company

Endorsements can also be done via Facebook updates, tweets, and videos. You should seek out local celebrities to use and endorse your products and services. This can work wonders for your business for an obvious reason. More people buy a product because a celebrity uses it (to follow the crowd) than because it has FDA approval.

Professional endorsement letters can multiply your business without the high cost or uncertainty of an advertising campaign.

ACTION STEP: Write down the names of five complementary businesses with clients similar to your best clients. Don't contact them today! Wait until you've read this book and improved your online and offline marketing. You only get one chance to make a great first impression.

Chapter 22

Effective Advertising

> The only purpose of advertising is to make sales. It is profitable or unprofitable according to its actual sales.
> —Claude Hopkins, *Scientific Advertising*

You can double your business without doubling your advertising budget. Impossible? No, you do this by making your advertising more effective. You'll find improving your advertising to be one of the best ways to leverage your marketing dollars. Why? An ad costs the same whether it brings in one call per day or ten calls per day. When you improve your ads, you'll get more calls and clicks without spending an extra dime on advertising.

Now take this pop quiz:

How do you define an effective advertisement?

A. You win a design award from AdWeek magazine.

B. Your friends and peers tell you how creative it is.

C. You get new clients and repeat business from it.

D. All of the above.

If you own an advertising agency, answers A and B are very important to you. If you are a service professional or business owner, then A is a distraction and B means you need to create a new ad. For ad agencies and sales reps, C is a terrifying answer because they don't want clients to think about results in terms of new clients and more sales. You should only care about C because you want to build your business and not your ego.

Reality check #1: Advertising agencies and ad reps get paid a commission on the volume of the ad buy. More ads purchased mean bigger commissions earned.

Reality check #2: Newspapers, magazines, and television stations won't give you a refund if your ad doesn't bring in prospects. That's your problem, not their problem.

I helped estate planning attorneys and financial planners publicize and present over 70 living trust seminars. We had a proven quarter-page newspaper ad which we ran three times before every seminar. The ads filled the seats. Even in a new city, our proven ads would result in a decent turnout. By running the same ad over months and years, we built familiarity, credibility, and attendance in the new city.

I am the managing partner in a business center which has an event center. Many aspiring business professionals rent the room, run an advertisement, buy food for their attendees, get dressed for success, and then no one shows up. What a disappointment for them. What a waste of money. This would not happen if the business had a proven and repeatable advertising program.

Creating an effective advertisement should not be guesswork. Copywriter Claude Hopkins analyzed ad results for decades to learn which ads worked and which ads flopped. Thousands of copywriters have studied his book *Scientific Advertising* since its publication in 1923.

Here are a few quotes from this classic advertising book:

"Almost any question can be answered, cheaply, quickly and finally, by a test campaign. And that's the way to answer them— not by arguments around a table."

"Ad-writers abandon their parts. They forget they are salesmen and try to be performers. Instead of sales, they seek applause."

"Don't try to be amusing. Money spending is a serious matter."

"Whenever possible we introduce a personality into our ads. By making a man famous we make his product famous."

"It is not uncommon for a change in headlines to multiply returns from five to ten times over."

"Some say, 'Be very brief. People will read but little.' Would you say that to a salesman?"

"The more you tell the more you sell."

"We try to give each advertiser a becoming style. He is given an individuality best suited to the people he addresses. To create the right individuality is a supreme accomplishment. Never weary of that part."

"Platitudes and generalities roll off the human understanding like water from a duck. Actual figures are not generally discounted. Specific facts, when stated, have their full weight and effect."

Being your own marketing consultant gives you a huge advantage over your competitors. You are learning how to create effective ads. Let your competitors waste money on say nothing/do nothing ads. You'll run ads to get more clients and sales. You'll replace gambling with your advertising budget to being scientific with your adverting. This means doing the following:

1. Create an effective ad based on proven techniques.

2. Test the ad with small or less widespread ads.

3. Track the results of the ad by tracking every lead.

4. Test small changes in the ad to improve results.

5. Expand your advertising campaign with your best ads.

When you know which ads consistently pull qualified prospects, you have created a lead machine for your business. A lead machine lets you bring in more leads when you need more business, like turning on a faucet when you need a drink of water.

Advertising great David Ogilvy once said, "Repeat your winners. If you are lucky enough to write a good advertisement, repeat it until it stops selling. Scores of good advertisements have been discarded before they lost their potency." Remember to keep running your effective ads, even after you grow tired of them, if they're still productive.

> **ACTION STEP: Gather together copies of your current and past advertising. Print out any online advertising. Keep them handy as you learn more about effective advertising in the pages ahead.**

Chapter 23

Image Advertising

> Half the money I spend on advertising is wasted; the trouble is I don't know which half.
> —John Wannamaker, 19th century retailer

Advertising can be divided into two categories: Image advertising and direct response advertising. We'll look at image advertising in this chapter and direct response advertising in the next chapter.

Bob Bly defines general or image advertising as "advertising that seeks to instill a preference for the product in the consumer's mind to promote the future sale of the product at a retail outlet or through a distributor or agent."

The key phrase in Bob's definition is "future sale" because the ad cannot generate an immediate sale. You recognize this easily because there is no call to action. Image advertisements focus on building awareness and positive feelings for the product or service.

Image advertising is seen every day in TV commercials for consumer products and magazines such as Forbes and Fortune for business-to-business advertising. Big companies spend big bucks shaping their brand image in the marketplace in hopes of making future sales. Sometimes it works, and sometimes it doesn't. Try to remember which companies spent millions of dollars to promote these slogans.

1. Your potential. Our passion.

2. Think outside the bun.

3. The power to be your best.

4. Drivers Wanted.

5. Have it your way.

Being your own marketing consultant lets you apply big company marketing like USPs to your company and reap the rewards. You should not copy big companies and spend your advertising budget on image ads. You simply can't afford it.

Here's an example. Many business owners place small display ads in their local newspapers and chamber magazines to "get their name out there." They often use the front side of their business cards. For the publication, these ads are easy to sell because of their small size. No extra graphic design work is needed, "Let's just use your business card." These little image advertisements get your name and contact information into the marketplace. However, there is no immediate reason for a reader to pick up the phone and call you or go to your website for a special report. You see the same thing with many full-page, full-color display ads.

The biggest problem with image advertising is not that they don't work. It's that image ads don't work immediately. You need more clients and sales now, not later. The second biggest problem with image ads is that you really don't know if the ad is helping your image or not. Or your sales. There is just no way to know. You need to know.

Advertising agencies make large commissions when big companies spend lots of money on major image advertising campaigns. Traditionally, advertising agencies got paid whether the ads work or not. Today, large companies are starting to demand results from their advertising. We'll see what happens.

These companies promoted the famous slogans listed above.

1. Microsoft
2. Taco Bell
3. Apple Computer
4. Volkswagen
5. Burger King

Millions of dollars got spent. Did you or anyone you know run out and buy their products based on these slogans?

Now let's look at a better way: Direct response advertising.

☐ **ACTION STEP: Look at your pile of past ads. How many are image ads?**

Chapter 24

Direct Response Advertising

> When I write an advertisement, I don't want you to tell
> me that you find it "creative." I want you to find it so
> interesting that you buy the product.
> —David Ogilvy, *Ogilvy on Advertising*

Image or indirect advertising may cause a prospect to buy your product or service down the road. Now let's look at "direct response advertising" which is a subset of direct response marketing.

Bob Bly defines direct response advertising as "advertising that seeks to get orders or leads directly and immediately rather than build an image or awareness over a period of time." This is the opposite of image or general advertising.

Direct response ads are easy to spot because they contain a call to action (CTA). The CTA can include a coupon to save money, an 800 number to order the product, or a link to a free report on a landing page. (A landing page is a special type of website we cover in Chapter 46.) These calls to action let you measure the response rate and know how well your ad is working.

You can use sales letters to get new clients. Jay Abraham wrote that a "sales letter can be used to develop a stream of prospects— prospects you then go out and visit, prospects you send further information or samples to, prospects who come to you, prospects you have to call, prospects you turn over to independent agents and manufacturers' reps. Direct mail can also be used to penetrate or access markets or prospects too small or distant to allow your customary form of selling or marketing to be effective."

You have a considerable advantage over professional copywriters. You know your target market well, and you know your products and services. You know what they want, and you know you can deliver it to them.

My wife Kathleen wrote a direct response sales letter in 2003. Our four daughters formed a bluegrass band called The Emmons Sisters when they were 9 to 15 years old. Kathleen wrote and mailed a simple letter to 25 retirement homes in our area. The offer was a live performance at $25 for 30-minutes and $50 for an hour. She had an 80% response rate because 20 called to book a date. Many became repeat clients. Her "secret" was mailing a compelling offer to a hungry market. You can do the same with direct mail. Please don't expect such a high response rate. 3-5% would be more typical. Repeat mailings to the same list would increase the total response rate.

You can turn an "image ad" into a direct response ad by offering readers a free report. Prospects call your office to get the report. You get their name and mailing address so that you can mail them the report. You should also ask, "Would you like to receive other helpful and interesting information via email?" You can mail them the report with a copy of your last physical newsletter or a product sample. Most importantly, you measure the success of your ad by knowing how many people called or clicked to get the report.

Here are other advantages of direct response advertising:

- **Testable:** You can change the headline or the offer and know if you improved or hurt the ad response.

- **Trackable:** You can insert a coupon code to know which ad attracted the customer.

- **Repeatable:** You can run proven ads and predict your results.

- **Action-oriented:** You ask your prospect to take action rather than let them passively look at an image ad.

Glitzy image advertising might win design awards. However, you want to win new clients. Direct response advertising causes prospects to contact your business now and get them into your marketing pipeline.

Make a big promise in your ads, and then deliver on your promise. Measure your results so you can test different ads against each other. Keep your winning ads, and drop the losers. Along the way, you'll build a strong company brand in the community based on the substance of your direct response ads.

Direct response advertising is testable, repeatable, and pays for itself. You'll learn how to create effective direct response ads in the next ten chapters.

> **ACTION STEP: In your pile of ads, determine how many are direct response ads.**

Chapter 25

The Easiest Way To Fix Your Ads

The most frequent reason for unsuccessful advertising is advertisers who are so full of their own accomplishments (the world's best seed!) that they forget to tell us why we should buy (the world's best lawn!).

—John Caples, *Tested Advertising Methods*

Whenever I want to improve a sales letter, yellow page ad, magazine ad, or web page, I first zero in on something easy to spot and simple to fix. Does the ad speak mostly about the business owner and his business? Or does it speak about what's in it for the client? What's the ratio of "I" and "mine" to "you" and "yours"?

Let me ask you a question: Are you reading this book to learn about me or learn how to grow your business?

My mom might read this book to learn something new about me. Maybe. The rest of you will read this book because you want to be unique in your marketplace, you want to get noticed by your prospects and your clients, and you want to double your business.

Seems so simple, but 99% of advertisers out there don't get this. It really is "all about you." I learned this in 1989 from marketing expert Jay Abraham. He taught me that everyone is tuned into the same radio station: WII-FM.

What does WII-FM stand for?

"What's In It For Me?"

My clients may like me, but they pay me money because they want to attract new prospects, improve their website, or have better looking and better working brochures.

Your prospects and clients don't really care about solving your problems. They really only care about solving or preventing their problems and getting what they want in life:

- Their retirement income: "Will I have enough?"
- Their financial goals: "When can I retire?"
- Their out-of-town guests: "Where should we go to eat?"
- Their impossible-to-buy-for mother-in-law: "Will she like it?"
- The best mechanic: "We can just rebuild that transmission."
- Their fear of not having the latest smartphone: "That's lame."
- His desire to impress her with a diamond ring: "Yes!"
- Parents with starving kids who want pizza now: "Domino's!"

Website Quick Fix Exercise

You can start your marketing makeover today with this exercise:

1. Print your website's homepage.

2. Put an "X" over every self-centered word such as "I".

3. Circle every client-centered word such as "You".

4. Count up the Xs and Os and compute your WII-FM ratio. If you have 14 "I" references and seven "You" references, then you have a 33% WII-FM ratio.

5. Now edit your copy to get your WII-FM ratio closer to 80% "You" and 20% "I".

6. With these changes, you'll improve your website's homepage.

You need to avoid the "I/my" approach in your marketing, or your prospects will avoid you.

Just between you and me, remember WII-FM in your marketing, and you'll find success.

> **ACTION STEP: Complete the website exercise above. Get extra credit by doing the same exercise with one of your current ads.**

Chapter 26

Creating Effective Ad Campaigns

Bait the hook to suit the fish, not the fisherman.

—Jerry Reitman

I must warn you of a major pitfall of being your own marketing consultant. As the business owner, you must not create ads from your perspective or to please yourself. You're already sold on your products and services, or you wouldn't be selling them. You know, like, and trust yourself, your company, and your products and services. In fact, you are so close to your products and services that you assume all the benefits must be obvious to the prospect. Not true. You must assume the opposite and educate your prospect on why your products and services can uniquely address your prospect's problem, want, or desire.

Let me put this another way because it's so important. You must create your ads from your prospect's perspective. You are the fisherman, and your prospects are the fish. Forget this, and your ad will underperform or outright fail to attract any new clients. Even worse, a poorly written ad might turn off existing clients.

You avoid this trap when you follow a systematic ad development process. You would do this if you were a marketing consultant helping someone else's business. Follow it for your own business, and your ads will bring in more clients and sales. You'll soon have ads you can count on to make the phone ring, people walk in your store, and buyers click on your links.

1. Determine the objective for your ad campaign. This could be filling seats at your next marketing seminar, announcing a Day-After-Christmas sale, promoting a new product or service, or generating attendance at some other special event.

2. Determine which of your target markets to focus on. For realtors, are you going after first-time homebuyers or empty nesters? One ad can't address both of these markets.

3. Now think of your avatar. This would be the avatar of the product or service to be sold in the ad. Your ad speaks to your avatar and her wants, fears, and/or desires. Let's call the avatar Stephanie. (We'll create your avatar in the next chapter.)

4. You create the ad for Stephanie, so your ad speaks to Stephanie and people like her. You want more clients like Stephanie, so your ad must speak to Stephanie to get people like her to take action.

5. You gather your market intelligence for this product or service. This includes past ads, testimonials, online reviews, complaint letters, brochures, buyer lists, and research.

6. You take this information and create your ad copy, i.e., words, following a proven ad structure. We'll cover this in Chapter 29.

7. Set aside your ad copy and let it "rest" for a few days. Get back to it with fresh eyes, and make it better. Remember your avatar. And forget about you.

8. Review your ad copy following the steps in Chapter 34.

9. Lay out your ad, following proven graphic design principles. You'll learn more about this in later chapters. Ad layout will differ greatly depending on your advertising medium: print, email, webpage, billboard, etc.

10. Test your ad with a small rollout. Because you track your ads, you'll know soon how well it is working.

11. A proven ad pays for itself with sales from new and repeat clients.

12. Roll out your proven ad with a larger ad purchase.

13. Keep running the ad even after you grow tired of it.

14. Occasionally test a new ad and try to beat your proven ad. In direct mail lingo, your proven ad is known as the "control."

☐ **ACTION STEP: Look at your pile of ads. Put your most successful ad on the top of the pile.**

Chapter 27

Know Your Market and Define Your Avatar

> Do not address your readers as though they were
> gathered together in a stadium. When people read your
> copy, they are alone. Pretend you are writing to each of
> them a letter on behalf of your client.
> —David Ogilvy, *Ogilvy On Advertising*

Being your own marketing consultant, you need to carefully consider who buys from you and why they buy. You know this much better after creating your unique selling proposition. You spoke with 20 of your best clients and learned why they do business with you. Now you want to create effective advertisements which will attract similar prospects to your business. To do this, you define an avatar for the product or service you wish to advertise.

An avatar represents a real or fictional person who you keep in mind at all times when creating an advertisement. Are you planning to send out 5,000 postcards? Or send out 5,000 emails? Either way, each will be read one at a time by individual people. An avatar helps you write your ads so they'll be read and acted upon.

Your avatar cannot be a blend of different types of prospects and clients. This becomes obvious when we imagine a used car salesperson working the lot.

A car salesperson talks to one prospect at a time. The prospect might be a college student who wants reliable transportation without a car loan. The prospect might be a married couple who want a safer and larger car because they just brought their first baby home from the hospital. The prospect could be a man about to celebrate his 50th birthday who wants a new car that makes him feel young again. These are three very different situations. Would a good car salesperson try to sell the same car to these three prospects? No, because a family sedan would be too expensive for the starving student, just right for the family, yet way too boring for the man wanting to feel younger. A good car salesperson will take a different approach with each of them.

Car manufacturers take the same approach in their advertising. Ford Mustangs and Ford pickup trucks require separate advertising campaigns. Local car dealership display ads often break up a big display ad into nine sections with mini-ads for different car types.

Depending on your business, you may have one or more avatars. First, you carefully define your avatar, and then you can create advertisements which appeal to your avatar. This process makes your advertisements more effective by touching specific needs rather than being generic.

80/20 Tip: You create your avatar understanding the demographics and psychographics of your 20% Clients.

Demographics refers to *who* buys from you. This means the age, sex, marital status, occupation, location, income, education, experience, hobbies, news sources, and outside activities of your ideal client. In the car example above, this could be a 19-year-old student, a young family, or a successful 49-year old business owner. The car salesperson can probably figure this out just by observing the prospect walk across the car lot.

Psychographics refers to *why* people buy from you or your competitors. This refers to the buyer's concerns in life, their fears, hopes, and dreams, what they love and what they hate, and past experiences which primed them to buy your products and services now or in the near future.

What causes them pain? Or gives them relief? What keeps them awake at night? What are their anxieties?

In our car example, the prospects wanted reliable and cheap, safe and roomy, or fun and youthful.

Carefully defining your avatar makes it much easier to create an effective advertisement. You use this analysis to define your avatar. Your avatar can be a real person, or it can be a composite of several top clients. Summarize your avatar into a 50- to 75-word paragraph. Give the avatar a name to make it personal.

With a carefully defined avatar, you'll be ready to start creating advertisements which will appeal to your avatar and motivate them to buy your product or service.

Without a carefully defined avatar, your ads will sound like so many real estate agents who claim to "specialize in commercial and residential real estate including homes, land, farms, and ranches for first-time homebuyers, growing families, and retirees ready to downsize for their golden years."

You greatly simplify the avatar creation process when you use a real person. Think of a person you know who desperately needs you and can afford to buy your products and services. Let's call her Christina. Perhaps you know her from your chamber of commerce or your church. She knows, likes, and trusts you. Yet for whatever reason, Christina hasn't purchased from you. She becomes your avatar. When you create your advertisements, you focus on persuading Christina to buy your products and services.

Whether real or imagined, your avatar defines your ideal prospect. You avoid generic sounding "please everyone and persuade no one" advertisements. You focus on your avatar, who represents your target prospect. Your avatar reflects your knowledge of your market. You specialize rather than generalize. Specialization leads to higher profits. Brain surgeons make more money than general practitioners. Remember this as you define your avatar.

⬜ **ACTION STEP: Study your market and define your avatar.**

Chapter 28

Seven Copywriting Basics

> To impress your offer on the mind of the reader or listener, it is necessary to put it into brief, simple language ... No farfetched or obscure statement will stop them. You have got to hit them where they live in the heart or in the head. You have got to catch their eyes or ears with something simple, something direct, something they want.
>
> —John Caples, *Tested Advertising Methods*

Being your own marketing consultant means knowing and applying the basics of copywriting. With better copy, you improve every sales letter, email, or text message you write. You create better advertisements, whether a display ad for a magazine or a script for a radio spot. Your response rates will go up, and you'll attract more of your desired clients. You won't be bedazzled by an advertising sales representative who focuses on glitz and image. Your ads will get better and better over time.

You don't need to invest thousands of hours to become a world-class copywriter like John Caples. You only need to be the best copywriter for your industry in your city. Since most plumbers, lawyers, and carpet cleaners know next to nothing about copywriting, this is much easier than it sounds. You'll learn enough copywriting in this book to improve your existing ads now. You can read additional books on copywriting later or just hire an experienced copywriter. Let's start with the basics.

Every ad consists of two basic parts, copy and graphic design. "Copy" refers to the words which make up an advertisement. Copywriters write ad copy. Graphic design refers to the layout and typology of the copy and the images which support the advertising message. Graphic designers create the ad layout. Advertising reps sell ads. (I repeat myself here to point out that the overwhelming majority of ad reps are neither copywriters nor graphic designers.) We start with copywriting and then cover graphic design. Let's begin with seven proven principles of good copywriting.

1. Copywriting is writing words which sell.

In 1905, John E. Kennedy famously observed that "advertising is salesmanship in print." He explained this to a young and junior partner of a Chicago advertising agency, Albert Lasker. Until that time, advertisements mainly presented dry, technical "news" about the products and services. Mr. Lasker hired Mr. Kennedy on the spot for 205 times what other copywriters were paid at the time. Working together they changed 20th century advertising philosophy and built the largest advertising agency in the world. How do you apply this? Your ads must not be boring lists of features. Your ads must sell.

Here's a copywriter's secret to jumpstart this process. Follow your best salesperson on a few sales calls either in person or on the phone. Next, record the sales pitch from introductions to closing the deal. You use a transcription of these recordings to write the first draft of your sales letter. This literal "salesmanship in print" approach prevents you from starting with a boring list of product or service features. This secret is very important, so I'll repeat it in the next chapter.

Writing words which sell means being specific rather than vague. Listing proof rather than empty claims. Using a client testimonial rather than just saying the same thing yourself.

There has been a long-running debate over long copy or short copy. Which works better?

At the Titans of Direct Marketing conference held in 2014, A-List copywriter Gary Bencivenga applied the 80/20 principle to this question. He explained how marketing studies showed that 20% of buyers bought 80% or more of products and services sold. These heavy users read long copy ads because of their high interest. Light users or uninterested prospects won't get past the headline. He wrote for these 20% high-users and found great success during his 50-year copywriting career. You can do likewise. A 60-second radio spot will sell more than a 30-second spot when you use the time wisely.

Attention spans are declining, so we're seeing more 15-second television ads now. Sometimes you have to get right to the point. However, there are 30-minute infomercials on my gym's TVs, so they must still work. Otherwise, the 1-800 numbers would stop ringing and the ads would stop running. Interested prospects will read your long-form advertisements.

You can combine long and short copy in your advertising using a two-step marketing approach. First, you grab your target prospect's attention with a short ad. This can be a small newspaper ad, Google AdWords, or 30-second television ad on your local cable station. You don't ask them to buy anything. You ask them to read your report before they buy anything from anyone. Your free report informs your prospect about their problem, provides a general solution, and tells them how to get this solution from your company. Next, you use long-form copy on a landing page, a free printed report, or a free consultation. During this second step, you try to make the sale.

For example, a real estate agent advertises a free report for first-time homebuyers. "The 7 Biggest Mistakes of First-Time Homebuyers and How to Avoid Them." In this ad, you don't ask to be their real estate agent. You only want them to read your report. You teach them things about home buying and mortgages which no one else told them. You position yourself as a trusted expert. At the end of the report, you invite them to take the next step: call to get their specific questions answered. When they call you, the sales process begins, and you ask to be their home-buying agent.

2. Forget What Your English Teacher Taught You!

To write effective copy, you need to forget some of the grammar rules you learned back in your school days. You're not writing a term paper or a doctoral thesis. You're writing to sell your product or your expertise to prospective clients, not to get an A on a paper.

This doesn't mean your ad should read like you wrote it with your thumbs. Don't be sloppy. Just don't get hung up over splitting infinitives or using "can't" instead of "cannot."

Here's a classic example of this copywriting principle.

Jeff Goodby of Goodby Silverstein & Partners created this famous slogan in less than a minute after seeing the ad images. Someone immediately asked, "Don't you mean: Do you have any milk?" His replied, "This is advertising, not a class in grammar."

You write to persuade, not impress. An old joke is that the best copywriters dropped out of school after the 5th grade. This way they never use complicated sentence structures, jargon, and seldom-used words. This book scored at the 7th-grade-level. You benefit because I wrote to be understood so you learn new skills and use them to grow your business.

The rules of English grammar are not the Ten Commandments. You can break grammar rules in the pursuit of persuasive communications. Your goal is more A-List clients, not an A+ grade and a smiley face.

Keep this in mind as we look at more copywriting basics.

3. Write How You Talk

If advertising is "salesmanship in print," then you need to write in an easy, conversational style. When you meet someone for the first time, you might say, "Hello, how are you doing today?" You pause and give them a chance to answer. The reader of your ad can't speak up. However, give the reader time to take a breath and take in what you're saying. You do this by writing short sentences and paragraphs.

How short? This short?

Yes.

If a sentence gets too long, put a period on it. Start a new sentence. When you finish your advertising masterpiece, test it by reading it out loud. If any part of it doesn't make sense, fix it. Give each sentence the "breath test." If you can't say a sentence in one easy breath, break it up so you can. Most people verbalize words in their heads when they read. Your ad copy needs to sound good to be effective.

Imagine if people spoke in traditional essay style: an introductory sentence, three sentences covering three points, and a concluding sentence. People don't speak like this, so don't write ads this way. Instead, write the way people in your target market speak. Got it?

4. Use Plain, Powerful Language

Don't write complex, compound sentences with pretentious language. Don't use a big, fancy word when a short, simple word gets your meaning across. Avoid jargon, or you'll make your reader feel stupid or ignorant. You won't impress them. However, you can educate them by explaining industry jargon in plain English. They'll appreciate this and may even thank you for it.

Avoid using the passive voice because it leads to weak copy. Passive voice uses the object as the subject. When you use the active voice, you give strength and power to your ideas. You should write plain declarative sentences—i.e., noun, verb, object.

Passive voice: "Saving for retirement is what Bob does."

Active voice: "Bob saves money for retirement."

Passive voice: "Packages are delivered to you on time."

Active voice: "Your packages arrive on time."

Passive voice: "Less gas is used by driving an electric hybrid car."

Active voice: "You use less gas driving an electric hybrid car."

Usually, using "is" as a verb means you're using the passive voice. Review your ad copy and get rid of the word "is." Other common uses are verbal phrases such as "are delivered" and "can be saved." Look for these types of phrases and change them to active voice. Your copy will pack more punch and power.

5. Remember Why People Buy

Never forget that people want to buy but don't want to be sold. Your copywriting needs to follow three simple rules of selling to do this.

First, you need to be gentle with prospects and avoid the hard sell. Imagine walking into a showroom of a used car dealership. A big talking, big smiling salesman charges toward you. You only wanted to take a look, and now it's "Look out!" Unlike in a car dealer showroom, your reader isn't trapped. Your prospect can toss your sales letter, click away from your website, or change the radio station. You should be friendly and gentle and help that prospect imagine solving a problem or reaching a goal.

Second, people make the buying decision for emotional reasons, not for logical reasons. Otherwise, why would anyone buy chocolate? Your words should appeal to people's emotional feelings and desires. Emotional feelings can be positive, such as the desire for gain. You can also use negative emotions, such as the fear of loss. For example, you can speak of spending more time with your grandchildren by having plenty of retirement funds. You evoke negative emotions by describing their "second career" as a Walmart greeter. In most cases, you'll find negative emotions evoke more action than positive emotions.

Even though a person makes the buying decision emotionally, you should provide them with a logical rationale for doing so. You include facts, figures, and guarantee reminders. You justify in their mind that they made the right decision. You see this in television ads for new cars which start out by showing a guy with a pretty girl in a convertible and finish with 32 miles-per-gallon and the 100,000-mile bumper-to-bumper warranty.

6. Be Opinionated and Be Personal

You want your ad to stand out from the crowd, so stand for something! Otherwise, why bother? Try to touch a nerve and get them to pay attention to you. You are a problem solver who can describe their problem in detail. Then describe how you can solve it and how they will feel without this problem in their lives any longer.

Your ad should sound like you wrote it to a specific couple and are speaking face-to-face with them. That's why you created your avatar in Chapter 27. You write your ad to your avatar so you "speak to her" and avoid generalities. Even if 10,000 people get your letter on the same day, each person reads it individually. Weave in a personal story, and your letter comes alive and becomes much easier to read. You'll be more persuasive and see better results.

7. Copywriting Is Hard Work

Yes, I used the passive voice for this one. Glad you noticed. Good copywriting is about selling and not simply following rules.

I learned copywriting by studying the great copywriters and by studying great sales letters and advertisements. For one course, I studied a subscription letter for *The Wall Street Journal* which produced over a billion dollars in revenue for Dow Jones. First, I had to read the letter ten times. Then I had to write it out by hand three times. My hand ached when I finished. These exercises taught me to write conversationally. I also understood why copywriters call this two-page sales letter "the most successful single piece of advertising in the history of the world." Yes, I include this ad with your book bonuses.

The hard work comes from researching your market, so you understand their fears, wants, and desires at a deep level. You speak to your market, not like a pushy salesperson, but as a helpful guide to help them reach their destination. Unlike a sales presentation, you can't respond to their questions, objections, or body language. You have to anticipate this and craft your ad copy to make the sale without being in the room. Write and re-write your ad copy until it sounds good spoken out loud as if by a salesperson with a prospect.

You have a huge advantage in being your own copywriter. No, you don't have the knowledge or experience of a full-time copywriter. However, you know and understand your market. Any hired copywriter would need to do a lot of homework to get to where you are today. You're already there.

Yes, it takes study and practice to learn effective copywriting and break old writing habits. You must learn to write plainly, clearly, and persuasively. By doing this, you improve the effectiveness of all your business communications. You'll get more sales without spending more money on advertising.

> **ACTION STEP:** Review your ads using these seven copywriting basics. Look for ways to improve your ads. You're training your marketing mind to write better ads in the future.

Chapter 29

Successful Advertising Formulas

> Whether one is now studying to go into the field of
> copywriting, whether he is new in the craft, or whether
> he has been a practitioner in it for years, his
> knowledge—and practice—of these fundamentals will
> determine the extent of his success.
> —Victor Schwab, *How To Write a Good Advertisement*

Let's review how you can improve your existing ads. In Chapter 25, you learned that your clients and prospects tune into WII-FM. They really don't care about you or your products or services. They only care about what's in it for them. Next, you learned seven copywriting fundamentals to help you think, feel, and write as a copywriter.

In this chapter, we'll look at several proven advertising formulas used to create effective ads. These advertising formulas include certain ad elements which we'll discuss in this and the following three chapters. You will use these proven ad formulas or frameworks to improve your existing ads and create better performing new ads.

You never have to start the ad creation process with a blank piece of paper. You'll start with the advertising formulas in this chapter. You will also start with two copywriter secrets to speed up your ad creation process.

First, begin with the words you or your top salesperson say to qualified prospects during successful sales presentations. Use your smartphone to record a sales presentation. Pay someone to transcribe the sales presentation. This starts the ad creation process with the sales flow and language of a successful sales presentation. A good sales presentation includes stories of similar clients helped in the past. Try to fit these words into an ad structure explained below. You won't have the back-and-forth conversation between the salesperson and the prospect. Instead, your copywriting must anticipate questions and provide answers in your ad. Finally, edit it down to fit the type of ad being created. This approach causes you to put "salesmanship in print" which eliminates the possibility of writing an ad like an 11th grade English paper.

Second, you can also create effective ads for your company by studying the ads of leading companies in your industry. I don't recommend copying ads from competitors in your local area. However, a dry cleaner in Denver can certainly borrow ad ideas from a successful dry cleaner in Dallas. You make them uniquely yours by including client testimonials and incorporating the uniqueness of your firm's products and services. You "reverse engineer" these successful ads to help learn how to create better ads for your company.

Now let's look at several proven advertising formulas.

Advertising Formulas

AIDA: Attention, Interest, Desire, and Action

I first learned about the "AIDA" formula in 1989 from marketing expert Jay Abraham. The AIDA structure has been used successfully for over a hundred years. AIDA is pronounced "eye-e-duh" in case someone asks.

AIDA stands for attention, interest, desire, and action. Your advertisement grabs your prospect's <u>attention</u> with a compelling headline, gets the prospect <u>interested</u> in your product or service, causes your prospect to <u>desire</u> your product or service, and finally asks the prospect to take <u>action</u> to buy your product or service.

You can remember the AIDA format by comparing it to a well-told story. A good story has a title (attention) so you know what it's about and gets you to start reading the book or watching a show. The story has a beginning (interest), middle (desire), and end (action). When a story has a boring beginning, you lose interest and read something else or flip the channel. That's why so many books and movies jump right into the action and use flashbacks later to tell the beginning of the story. Finally, the story ends with an exciting or surprising conclusion. Cliffhangers cause you to watch the next episode or read the next book in the series.

Victor Schwab's Five Advertising Fundamentals

Victor Schwab wrote the book *How To Write a Good Advertisement* which was published in 1962. His five advertising fundamentals form a five-step selling sequence for writing a good advertisement.

1. Get Attention.
2. Show People an Advantage.
3. Prove It.
4. Persuade People to Grasp the Advantage.
5. Ask for Action.

Attention, Image, Action

You see this structure on billboards because there is so little room or time for a lot of words. Billboards need an attention-getting headline, a picture which draws out a key emotion (fear, greed, want), and then a call to action. The call to action can be a phone number or a website address. Keep it short and simple.

Problem, Solution, Action

Boardroom Books used this three-step ad structure for many years. Problem, Solution, Action. This ad structure works well on flyers or anywhere you have to limit your words.

You can't just name the problem in the headline. You need to pour a little salt in the wound to aggravate the situation. Next you offer your product or service as the solution to their problem. Use bullets and testimonials here. Finally, you provide a call to action to help them buy your solution to their problem.

Dan Kennedy tweaked this formula into problem, agitate, solution. He says that "When you understand that people are more likely to act to avoid pain than to get gain, you'll understand how powerful this first formula is ... It may be the most reliable sales formula ever invented."

You agitate their problem by highlighting the emotions (pain, fear, regret) that go with this problem.

Advertisement Structure Elements

Now let's look at advertising elements common to most successful advertisements. You won't find every one of these elements in every advertisement. The ad medium determines how much can be said or shown in an ad.

Pre-head

In print ads, this is the small type at the very top of the ad. In radio ads, it's the first few words of the ad. You want to cut through the clutter and get your target audience to pay attention.

I've run radio ads with this pre-head, "Attention Business Owners!" I do this because I want business owners to pay attention to the rest of the ad. Employees, retirees, and teenagers can tune out or change the radio station. I don't care about them. The ad is not directed at them. More examples:

If you're selling pet supplies, you say "Attention Dog Lovers!"

If you're a financial advisor, you say "Attention Investors!"

If you're a mortgage broker, you say "Attention Homeowners!"

If you're a real estate agent, you say "Attention Renters!"

Did you notice that I used a pre-head on the cover of this book? "Local Business Success Series." This pre-head targets my intended audience and sets this book apart from other marketing books.

Headline

Your headline is the "ad for the ad." You grab your prospect's attention with a powerful headline. When you fail here, they won't read or listen to another word of your ad.

Depending on the advertising medium, a stunning photograph can also be used to grab the attention of the reader. We'll cover this in Chapter 37 on using graphic design to create effective ads.

People are bombarded with more ads than ever before, every day. Just how many ads are seen by a typical American today? I've read estimates of 5,000 to 30,000 ad impressions per day. This is far above the average of 500 ads per day in the 1970s. This means an attention-getting headline is now more important than ever.

You'll learn how to create effective headlines in the next chapter.

Lead

The "lead" refers to the lead paragraph following the headline. You must get right to the point and bring the headline to life. Are you offering improvement or telling how to eliminate a problem? Leads can be indirect or direct.

Your lead can begin with a story which speaks indirectly to your prospect. You put your prospect in someone else's shoes who has the same problem or desire for improvement. Life insurance companies use an indirect approach when they tell a story of the unexpected death of the family's breadwinner. Restaurants can tell the story of a couple celebrating their 25th wedding anniversary.

When you're selling to your clients, you can be more direct. No need to waste their time. They know who you are. You can be more direct and jump right into your offer. Imagine a wine shop saying, "We ordered ten cases of Merlot, and they sent 20. The next ten cases will go for 40% off because we don't have room in our warehouse."

The goal of the lead is to get your prospect to keep reading your ad. You do this by keeping their attention with a compelling story or the promise of a great deal.

Credibility

At this point, your prospect knows you offer a solution to their problem. Now you must answer the question, "Why should I trust you to solve my problem?" You only mention qualifications relevant to your prospect. This can include education, experience, or certifications of you and your employees. Your goal here is to show why you and your company are qualified to solve their problem as highlighted in the ad. Not to tell your life story. You can tell more about you and your company on your website "About" page. Not in your ad.

You can also add social proof by including a list of local companies which use your services. You can use local company logos to get the same effect.

Have you spoken on local radio talk shows? In this case include, "As heard on KAJO radio." The same thing is true if you write a column for your local newspaper. If you do this and it's relevant to your prospect, mention it in your ad.

Testimonials

You can claim to solve the problem or provide the benefit promised in the headline. Your prospects may believe you, or they may not believe you despite your claims of credibility. Client testimonials provide third-party verification of your ability to do the same thing for your prospect.

The best testimonials are video testimonials of well-known people in your community. I've used audio testimonials in radio ads. Why say it yourself when you can get a client to say it for you? Written testimonials with a picture and client name work in print ads and on websites. Written testimonials without a picture or name also work but have less credibility because they are easy to fake.

The power of testimonials comes from your prospects walking in the shoes of your clients from the time they had the problem to the time you solved the problem.

Bullet Points

Bullets are brief statements containing a single benefit of your product or service. Bullets provide "what" and "why" about a product or service without providing the "how" it does it. Your prospect needs to buy your product or service to learn "how" to solve their problem or get what they want.

Here are more advantages and uses of bullets:

- Bullets help build interest and desire in your prospect.
- **Bullets can include research, testimonials, and proof.**
- Bullets can answer questions in your prospect's mind, so they are ready to buy.
- **Bullets let you remove reasons *not to buy*.**
- Bullets let prospects scan your copy for key benefits without reading the whole ad.

Solution

At this point, you make clear that your prospect really has only one way to get the benefit or solve their problem. The prospect must buy your product or service. FedEx did this nearly 40 years ago when you absolutely, positively had to have your letter delivered the next day. The post office was not an option.

Victor Schwab wrote how to help your prospect grasp the advantages of your product or service:

> One of the key methods is to sum up the emotional and logical reasons your prospect should buy, then help them picture themselves already enjoying the benefits of your product or service. Once your prospect is already imagining himself--and the life he'll have when he has your product—he'll be especially eager to buy it.

After you make claims for your product or service, you need to prove your claims. Victor Schwab wrote that,

> Most people will not believe what you tell them in an ad, unless you prove it with facts, figures, testimonials, scientific proof, and any other method you can devise. Here's a huge secret. Whilst most prospects will buy for deeper emotional reasons, they want to justify their purchase with hard facts. That's where proof becomes especially valuable. Proof also helps build belief in your prospect fueling those emotional desires to buy. Whilst we might believe that we buy on logic—the truth is, the heart dictates to the head when it comes to most of our buying decisions.

Offer

What are you offering to do? What will your prospect get? What's the main benefit of your product or service? How much will it cost in time and money? What happens if it doesn't work out?

Answers to these questions make up your offer. The remaining ad elements together make up your offer. We'll spend more time on defining your offer in Chapter 31.

Price

Now you get to the price of your product or service. You must resist competing on price if you want to escape the rat race and enjoy your life. Otherwise, you'll need to sell a lot more to make the same amount of money. Let me give you a quick example for this.

Bob is a contractor who generally makes a 20% profit on his remodeling jobs. A potential client wanted him to slice 10% off a $100,000 project. If Bob agreed, he would gain a client but lose $10,000 of his normal $20,000 profit. At this lower profit margin,

Bob would need to double his sales to make the same overall profit. That would entail hiring more employees and growing his overhead. His business would be more complicated, less profitable, and less fun.

Price should not be an issue if you've made the case that your product or service is the only way they can solve their problem or get the promised benefit. Our contractor Bob is known in his city as the only remodeling contractor who guarantees no cost overruns (his USP). Bob can hold firm on his price, because the prospect can only get this peace of mind buying from Bob.

FedEx got $10 per letter instead of a 25-cent stamp. Price really didn't matter if your contract absolutely, positively had to be on your prospect's desk tomorrow. That's what effective advertising can do for you as well. Again, don't compete on price.

Guarantee

Your guarantee removes the risk of your prospect taking action. Your prospect feels safe buying your product or service because you take the fear away. FedEx guaranteed delivery by 10:30 AM or you got your money back.

Many businesses can make strong guarantees. However, heavily regulated industries such as financial planning cannot make any promissory guarantees. In this case, you make a quasi-guarantee: "Guaranteed to make you think!" Or "I guarantee to answer your questions in plain English."

Takeaway

You need to create a real sense of urgency in your prospect's mind. You can offer a special early-bird special or bonus limited by quantity or a deadline date. Retailers have said for decades, "Shop early for best selection." If you are a service professional, you have limited appointments available for new clients. Even FedEx had a drop-off deadline if you wanted your package to be delivered tomorrow.

Call To Action

You summarize your offer, ask for the order, and tell them how to get it. You must make this very clear to the prospect. This could be calling your office, clicking a link, or coming to your store for a Black Friday sale.

Don't leave your prospect guessing or confused about what to do next. As information marketing strategist Fred Gleeck says, "A confused mind doesn't buy."

P.S. Printed sales letters and client letters and online website landing pages can and should include a P.S. Studies show it is the second most-read element of sales letters after the headline. Repeat your offer with a sense of urgency and tell them how to take action.

In the next few chapters, you'll learn more about how to improve your ad headlines and your offers. When you improve your headlines, more people will read your ads. When you improve your offers, more prospects will buy your product or service. This 80/20 approach can quickly improve your ads and increase your sales.

> **ACTION STEP: Write an ad using this simple three-part ad structure.**
>
> 1. Problem (Headline and lead paragraph)
>
> 2. Solution (Product and service benefits and offer)
>
> 3. Call to Action (How to get it)

Chapter 30

Grab Attention with Your Headline

> The headline contains an important consumer benefit, or news, or arouses curiosity, or promises a reward for reading the copy.
>
> —Bob Bly, *The Copywriter's Handbook*

Without a powerful and persuasive headline, your ad copy won't be read. Your offer won't be considered. You'll waste your money.

What should a good headline do? In *The Copywriter's Handbook* (pages 16-21), Bob Bly describes the four functions of a headline:

1. **Get attention.** This gets the reader to read more of the ad.

2. **Select the audience.** Who do you want to attract? Who would you rather not attract?

3. **Deliver a complete message.** David Ogilvy, author of *Confessions of an Advertising Man*, says that 80% of readers will only read the headline, so give them a complete sell. Ogilvy's Century 21 ad was "You Can Make Big Money in Real Estate Right Now."

4. **Draw the reader into the body copy.** The promise of solutions to current or potential problems gets the reader to continue reading more of the ad.

Let's consider these four functions as we look at a few headlines.

"How to Win Friends and Influence People"

Dale Carnegie wrote this best-selling book in the 1930s. Copywriter Victor Schwab used the book's title as the headline for ads selling the book. The headline grabs the reader's attention and builds curiosity, because who doesn't want more friends? Who doesn't want more influence? This headline does #1 and #4. It also selects the audience (#2) because everyone wants more friends.

"Did Your 401(k) Become a 201(k)?"

This headline grabbed attention (#1) by dramatizing a 50% fall in the stock market. It selected the audience (#2) by assuming the reader had a 401(k). It pulls the reader into the copy (#4) because it implies a solution to the problem of a falling retirement portfolio. While powerful, it missed on #3 by not offering a solution to the problem. You don't need to get four out of four to have a winning headline.

"Worried About Outliving Your Retirement Funds?"

This headline grabs attention (#1) by highlighting the pain of running out of money during retirement. It selects the audience (#2) advisors want to reach because pre-retirees and retirees worry about this; 25-year-olds don't give it a thought. It can't deliver a complete message (#3) because the problem will differ greatly from person to person. The headline raises a real concern during times of rising consumer prices and low interest rates to draw the reader into the rest of the ad (#4).

The most common headline mistake is using the company name as the headline. Never forget WII-FM. Your prospects don't care about the name of your company. They care about solving their problems and getting what they want. Use a powerful and compelling headline, and you'll have much more effective ads. Why? Because your prospects will keep reading your ad or listening to your radio spot.

The "Knock-Knock" Headline Test

You can evaluate your headlines with a headline test developed by a major ad agency many years ago. You imagine selling your product or service door-to-door to homeowners or business owners. You know the neighborhood or office building is full of qualified prospects. Here's the test:

1. You knock on the door.

2. Your prospect is standing there.

3. You say your headline to your prospect.

4. Did you get invited in or not? That's the test.

Because advertising is "salesmanship in print," this headline test is really the "door-to-door salesperson's opening line in print."

I sold attic insulation door-to-door during the summer of 1980. I was a junior in college. This was a time of high fuel bills, and the price of everything was going up. I worked between 4:00 PM and 8:00 PM Monday through Friday. I knew I had one chance to get the homeowner's attention or they'd say, "No, thank you," and close the door.

I did not say, "Hi. I'm selling attic insulation. Would you like to find out how much it costs?" I also did not say, "Hi, I work for XYZ Insulation Company," because they didn't care about the name of my company. I used WII-FM without realizing it.

I asked with a smile, "Hi. Would you like to learn about a gas company program to save you money on your gas bill?" Sometimes no one was home, or a renter answered the door. Otherwise, this opening line usually got me into the house. My opening line could have been the basis of an effective headline:

New Gas Company Program Saves You Money On Your Gas Bill

I wish I had this book when I was 20 years old. I would have created a flyer with this headline to get leads for selling more attic insulation. I would have left it on the doormat of every home where no one was home. Oh well, we live and learn, and then we earn. Now let's learn more about the importance of having a good headline for your advertisements.

When you write better headlines, you improve the results of every advertisement, flyer, invitation, press release, client letter, and email you write. A good headline means more prospects buying whatever you are selling. "Buying" can mean opening an email message, watching the rest of your TV ad, listening to your radio ad, reading your newspaper advertisement, buying your product or service, clicking a link, or registering for your community seminar.

Ted Nicholas became famous with his bestselling book, *How To Form Your Own Corporation Without A Lawyer for Under $50*. He spent hundreds of millions of dollars selling millions of books primarily through full-page ads in national magazines and major newspapers including *The New York Times* and *The Wall Street Journal l*. Ted tested every aspect of his ads to maximize his marketing return on investment. Ted learned that "73% of the buying decision is made at the point of the headline." 80/20 thinking means spending the majority of your energy on the ad's headline. When Ted wrote a $100,000 check to a magazine, he knew he had a great headline on a winning ad.

I have benefited greatly by studying his work. When Ted talks, I listen. You should too. Consider Ted's view on headlines:

> Based on hundreds of tests conducted, a good headline can be as much as 17 times more effective than a so-so headline. And this is with exactly the same body copy!

Ted recommends writing the headline first before writing any other part of an ad. He begins the headline creation process by listing every possible benefit. How will this product or service help the buyer? Based on his avatar, he ranks the benefits in order of importance. Next, he turns these benefits into headlines and writes as many as he can think of. Sometimes as many as 200 for one product! Once you've settled on the main headline, you can start putting together the rest of the ad. You can use the "runner-up headlines" as subheads and bullets to highlight other advantages of your product or service.

Remember that your headline must speak to a want, need, or desire of your prospective client. This is the biggest benefit that your product or service offers.

Seven Headline Templates

Now let's look at seven ways to write effective headlines.

1. The How-To Headline

Add the words "How To" to your current headline, and you'll get better results. Ted Nicholas ran the same ad with only these two words added to the headline and increased results by 17%. I did this with a headline for living trust seminars flyers and newspaper ads. We had a proven ad with this headline:

Avoid Probate With a Living Trust

I improved the results by adding these two little words:

How To Avoid Probate With a Living Trust

People are looking for solutions to their problems. The "How to" headline draws them in because they want to know "how to" do something, get something, or solve a problem.

2. The Curiosity Headline

You can offer to fill a gap in the marketplace with the words "Finally," or "At Last, You Can…" These headlines build curiosity because you may solve a problem they've had for a long time.

> **At Last, You Can Stop Worrying About Your Health**

or

> **Finally, Business Owners Multiply Sales Without Hiring an Expensive Marketing Consultant**

3. Just Say Yes

Everyone hears "No" so often from parents, teachers, and bosses that hearing "Yes" stops people in their tracks.

> **Yes, You Can Double Your Sales Without Doubling Your Advertising Budget**

Yes, I learned this from Ted Nicholas.

4. The Testimonial Headline

A client testimonial creates a strong headline by adding credibility and personalizing the product or service. Here's a classic "testimonial" type ad written by copywriting legend John Caples:

> **"They Laughed When I Sat Down At the Piano—But When I Started to Play!"**

John Caples was an old-school copywriter long before the Federal Trade Commission (FTC) came on the scene. The FTC frowns on fake testimonials, so create this type of headline using actual testimonials, not merely something you wished a client would say. You can combine several testimonials into a composite testimonial. Put the testimonial in quotes to improve your headline further.

Let me adapt this classic headline into a quasi-testimonial for this book:

> **"They Laughed When I Became My Own Marketing Consultant— But When I Doubled My Business!"**

Your competitors won't know you've doubled your sales. However, they will notice when you take a long vacation. Hence this version:

"They Laughed When I Became My Own Marketing Consultant— But When I Took a European Vacation!"

5. The Question Headline

When you ask a question in your ad's headline, interested readers will read the rest of your ad to find the answer.

Tired of Waiting For the Phone To Ring?

Do you think retired people would read this ad? Definitely.

Worried About Running Out of Retirement Money?

6. Include "Free" and "New"

These two words are proven to grab attention.

Free Special Report On Avoiding the 5 Most Common Wedding Planning Mistakes

People are interested in learning about new solutions to old problems.

Discover 7 New Ways To Hire Better Employees

Both of these headlines have a number in them. For some reason, odd numbers of lists work better. The exception to this rule is "Top 10" lists which work well.

7. Hidden Benefit Headline

The other six headline types touch on obvious benefits to your prospect. You can dig deeper and uncover a "hidden benefit" of your product or service.

Ted Nicholas used "The Ultimate Tax Shelter" as the headline for selling 200,000 copies of his book on setting up your own corporation. This single ad generated over $4 million in book sales. Yet the book itself didn't use the phrase "tax shelter." He says that the "tax shelter possibilities are why many people form corporations." This was the hidden benefit.

When you see the same ad running again and again in your local paper or in a magazine, you know it must be working. Remember, a great headline is the number one reason an ad will work again and again. Folks see the ad, read the headline, then read the rest of the ad, and finally take action.

Now take another look at your own ads and see how you can improve your headlines. Be sure to use the "Knock-Knock test" we covered above to test your headlines.

After you replace most of the "I, me, and mine" with "You and your," the next best way to improve your existing ads is by improving the headline.

> **ACTION STEP: Write some headlines for your business using the headline types explained in this chapter. Get a little crazy, and remember to speak to your avatar.**

Chapter 31

Define Your Offer

Make an offer they can't refuse.

—John Caples

You created a unique selling proposition for your business in Part 2. You answered Dan Kennedy's question from your prospects:

"Why should I choose your business/product/service versus any/every other competitive option available to me?"

For many brick-and-mortar businesses, your USP should be included on every marketing piece. Your USP is not a complete offer but does support your offer and helps you build your reputation. For example, we looked at a financial advisor's USP in Chapter 17. Here it is again:

Finally, Plain English Answers to Your Retirement Questions

Your offer must appeal to your market's biggest pain points, fears, and desires and offer the best solution to your market's pain, fears, and desires. Ideally, you offer the only solution to this problem or want in your city. Your offer includes every valuable and irresistible thing your client receives in exchange for their money.

You find out what people in your market want, and you offer it to them. Your complete offer will tell your prospects what makes the product or service different and more valuable from what they use now. Your offer describes the payment terms, delivery options, and guarantees.

Your offer should also give the reasons why you are making a special deal possible. A furniture retailer can offer 50% off. Why such a huge discount? A pending bankruptcy would make any guarantee worthless. Or a broken water heater forced them to move all furniture into the parking lot while new flooring is installed. Big difference.

Your offer will differ depending on the advertising medium. Google Ads can change hourly. Yellow pages ads run all year long, so your call to action must make sense year around. For instance, carpet cleaners could offer a free report related to the problems of dirty carpet. You can see this technique in action by a San Francisco area carpet cleaner. The website offers several free reports about carpet cleaning. Here's one: "Insider's Guide to Carpet Cleaning gives simple methods and detailed strategies to avoid the common misconceptions about having a clean healthy carpet!"

Source: therugexpert.com/Free_Report_Consumer_Guide.html

An advertisement for a no-obligation tax planning analysis would work during tax season. A newspaper ad for a free community seminar will only work a week before the event.

Your offer will differ depending on your type of business. Feel free to borrow marketing ideas from other industries. Something common in one industry can be innovative in another.

Service Professionals

We used to differentiate between white-collar and blue-collar service professionals. Now financial advisors and attorneys wear blue shirts, while contractors wear white shirts with Home Depot logos. Oh well. The sales process is different, so offers will vary.

Service professionals such as CPAs, attorneys, insurance agents, financial advisors, engineers, estheticians, and consultants have a common marketing goal: Get the prospect into their office for a free consultation. Second best is to have the prospect call your office for more information. These types of professionals seldom sell anything directly online or offline to a customer. Each offer of service should match the particular needs of the prospect.

You can make an offer to send a free report by email or snail mail, invite them to a community marketing seminar, or call now to set an appointment.

At The Boardroom, my entire marketing program has one objective: Get the prospect to come in for a tour to see available offices, stand in the conference rooms, and experience The Boardroom in person. Once in the door, the marketing process ends, and the sales process of matching their needs to what we offer begins.

The same thing is true for you if you're a service professional.

Your goal is to make it easy and low-pressure for a prospect to come in for this initial meeting. For living trust seminars, our ad said, "This meeting is free, and there is no pressure to buy anything." At The Boardroom, I changed "come in for a tour" to "come in and take a look" because it sounds more casual and less pressured.

Emergency Service Professionals

Many "blue-collar" service professionals serve clients with immediate needs. People with a stopped-up kitchen sink don't want to attend a community seminar about plumbing or read a free report. They want someone to unplug their sink, and now. In this case, your ad can offer 24/7 emergency service with no upcharges for holidays. Ideally, you're associated with other plumbers to avoid "being on call" for every weekend and holiday.

Emergency room doctors also fall into this category. Urgent care clinics often cost far less than hospitals. The same is true for clinics offering elective surgery. You need to let potential patients know why you're a better choice than going to the big hospital in town. Here is how one such clinic markets itself in my town:

> **"Grants Pass Surgery Center provides a more convenient, affordable, and personalized approach to outpatient surgery."**

Offer Free Services as a Hook

Many service professionals offer a free and valuable service to establish expertise and build trust with a prospect.

Real estate agents offer free broker price opinions in hopes of getting the home sale listing. This offer doesn't work as well as it used to, because too many brokers tell homeowners what they want to hear: a high list price.

One local company in my city offers free home inspections to improve air quality and cut heating and cooling bills. The goal is to improve the energy efficiency of homes with better insulation and modern windows.

Retail Stores

Retail stores can make general offers like "Labor Day Sale This Weekend!" as well as specific offers for particular items on sale. Your offer describes the merchandise selection, free delivery and setup, and return policies.

Don't make people do math. Show the value saved in dollars. "Save 20%" is vague. "Save $200 on this $1,000 couch" is specific and memorable.

Retail stores can also offer special deals to existing clients only. This type of offer will be appreciated by your clients who want to be treated special. They ought to be, since they supported your business in the past.

Here is one more thing to avoid in your offers. Don't treat prospects better than your clients. This happens when your local cable company mails you a postcard offering a great deal for "New customers only." This is an example of how poor advertising can cause you to lose customers. Do the opposite. In copywriter Dick Benson's words, "A special discount to customers as compared to outsiders will increase response by more than the discount."

The final part of your offer is the "call to action." Without this, you won't make the sale. We'll cover this in the next chapter.

> **ACTION STEP: Can you say your main offer in 20 seconds? Would it get my attention and make me want to find out more? Write it down. Practice it.**

Chapter 32

A Call To Action To Close the Sale

> If life is primarily about action, then copywriting is the
> communications medium that prompts action in others.
> —David Garfinkel, *Breakthrough Copywriting*

You grabbed your prospect's attention with a strong headline. You kept her reading or listening with a strong lead paragraph. You got her interested in your product or service with benefits backed up with proof. She wants your product or service. Now you need to close the sale by writing the "close" at the end of your ad. The close is also known as the "call to action."

Your prospect must take action for you to make the sale. Victor Schwab compared good and bad ads this way:

> One advertisement will cause readers to comment upon its being
> well written, attractive, and convincing. Another advertisement
> will not only capture attention, hold interest, and win conviction
> ... but also get action.

In *Advertising for Immediate Sales*, John Caples reminds us that advertising is salesmanship in print. This is especially true when the copywriter is trying to close the sale:

> There are a lot of good advertisements that are weak in the final
> urge to act. They are like salesmen who are charming talkers but
> weak closing men. If they had the right stuff they would pick the
> reader up by the collar of his coat and the seat of his trousers and
> stiff-arm him into a showroom.

You need to tell your prospect exactly what to do to buy your product. You need to make it simple, easy, and specific.

Most important of all, the call to action in your sales copy needs to get your prospect to act NOW. Any delay and you'll likely lose the sale altogether.

Your call to action should be a simple, clear, and urgent call to your prospect to take action: Either buy the product or service, or take the next step in the sales cycle.

"Call our office today at 333-444-5555 to receive your free report."

"Visit our website for free retirement planning calculators and dozens of free reports."

"Seating is limited, so please call 1-800-111-2222 to reserve your seat."

"Bring in this coupon to get a free appetizer with your meal."

"Click the Buy Button to gain immediate access to ...."

"Click this link to get your free report ...."

"Use the enclosed reply card and envelope to order your...."

At the bottom of your ad, you can include your company name, address, and contact information. Make it easy to read so they can take action and reach you. Don't make them hunt for your phone number, contact page, or chat box. Make it easy for them to order, and you'll make more sales.

ACTION STEP: Write out the call to action for your main offer.

Chapter 33

Why Track Your Ads?

Do not depend on opinions. Use some kind of objective test to determine the relative effectiveness of advertisements.

—John Caples, *Tested Advertising Methods*

For most small business owners, the most popular form of gambling is advertising. These businesses waste tons of money on advertising because the owner has no idea if the ad is working or not. It doesn't have to be this way.

By tracking your ads, you gain a huge advantage over your competitors. You stop running ads which don't generate new and repeat clients. You run proven ads on proven ad platforms. Your ads get predictable and repeatable results so you can outspend your competitors.

However, the only way to know which ads are working is to include a tracking mechanism. This can be a coupon, special phone number, or a special landing page for a pay-per-click ad.

Tracking your ads lets you test your ads. The classic book on testing ads is John Caples, *Tested Advertising Techniques*. He writes,

The key number was an invention that has done as much for the science of advertising as the X-ray has done for the science of medicine. It has made it practical, simple, and inexpensive to know exactly how many inquiries or how many sales came from each advertisement. The importance of this is far-reaching. It is one of the greatest steps ever made toward taking the guesswork out of advertising.

Victor Schwab used coupons in his ads so he could link every sale to a particular ad. He used them to test new headlines, stories, images, offers, and guarantees and know which ads worked best.

You must know the source of every lead. You must know which ads are working and which ones need to be improved or discarded. In addition to tracking codes in ads, you should also train your employees to ask first-time callers and visitors, "How did you find out about us?"

When you track your ads, you can work on improving them. You stick with your winners and spend money on advertising with confidence. You can test new ads on a small basis and roll them out after you know they will at least pay for themselves. No more gambling with your advertising budget!

Ad tracking also lets you compute marketing return on investment ("MROI") using your sales revenue and advertising costs.

Service companies: MROI = (sales − costs) / costs

Product companies: MROI = (gross margin − costs) / costs

Let's calculate the marketing return on investment for a financial advisor hosting a living trust seminar.

He spends $10,000 on advertising, food, and venue expenses.

He gets new clients who together have one million dollars to invest.

He nets 2% on new money invested, which is $20,000 for this seminar.

MROI = ($20,000 - $10,000) / $10,000

MROI = 100%

This simple calculation understates total MROI because it excludes future income from these seminar attendees. We look at this again in Chapter 44 when we cover lifetime value of clients.

Without ad tracking, there is no way to compute MROI for individual ads.

If the number of clients is small and in-person, you can track ad performance by asking, "How did you find out about us?" At marketing seminars, you can ask the audience to raise their hands. "Did you hear about this seminar from the newspaper ad?" "How about radio?" "How about my blimp? Just kidding, let's get started." You learn what works well and do more of it for future seminars.

You can also quiz ad reps with this question, "What's your favorite way to track ad performance?" They may squirm a bit. The best ones will give you a plain English explanation. The better ones will ask you for an explanation. An honest one will look baffled and ask you what you mean. The worst ones will leave quickly to find business owners who appreciate glitzy image ads.

> **ACTION STEP:** Look at your pile of ads. How many track results? None? Good, you now have another way to improve your ads.

Chapter 34

How to Review Your Copywriting

> Copywriters are salespeople whose job is to convince people to buy products.
>
> —Bob Bly

When I started out as a marketing consultant, I wrote the ad copy and did the graphic design. You may choose a more traditional route by writing the ad copy and then hiring a graphic designer to lay out the ad. In my case, my wife eventually used her art background to learn computer graphic design.

This was a big help for me because I could focus on what I do best (the words), while she focused on what she did best (the layout and images). I recommend you do the same thing, because copywriting and graphic design are two completely different professions.

This means you must review your ad copy carefully before you hand it over to the graphic designer. First, review the copy for spelling, grammar errors and accuracy. Next, you review the copy as a copywriter. Will it be an effective ad? Here's how to do this.

Bob Bly has been a professional copywriter for over 30 years. Before he gives ad copy to his client or a graphic designer, he reviews the copy using his copywriter's checklist. He explains this in detail on pages 61-62 of *The Copywriter's Handbook*. Here are his ten questions with my comments in parentheses.

1. Does the copy fulfill the promise of the headline? (or "bait and switch" the reader)

2. Is the copy interesting? (or boring)

3. Is it easy to read? (or scholarly, jargon-filled, or incoherent)

4. Is it believable? (or unbelievable)

5. Is it persuasive? (or only informative)

6. Is it specific? (or general)

7. Is it concise? (or wordy)

8. Is it relevant? (Remember WII-FM)

9. Does it flow smoothly? (or is it choppy and disjointed)

10. Does it call for action? (or leave the reader wondering, "What do I do next?")

You should use this checklist to review your current and future advertisements. You'll see better results and avoid embarrassing and expensive mistakes such as forgetting to ask your prospect to call, click, or come to your store.

You can also use John Caples' seven-step checklist to successful ads to improve your copywriting.

1. Does your advertisement attract the RIGHT AUDIENCE?

2. Does your ad HOLD the audience?

3. Does your copy CREATE DESIRE?

4. Do you prove it's a BARGAIN?

5. Do you establish CONFIDENCE?

6. Do you make it EASY TO ACT?

7. Do you give prospects a reason to ACT AT ONCE?

Finally, make a habit of reading your copy out loud again and again during the editing process. Your copy becomes more conversational to your prospects when it sounds better to your ears. Your eyes alone scan over clunky sentences which sound ugly to your ears. Do this before you give your ad copy to your graphic designer, and you'll save money on graphic design fees.

In the next chapter, you'll start a crash course in graphic design.

☐ **ACTION STEP: Review your best current advertisement using the tests in this chapter. Discover ways to improve this ad, and start rewriting it.**

Chapter 35

Your Crash Course in Graphic Design

Graphic design is conveying a message visually. Whether it's a TV commercial, website, or sales letter, graphic designers make the message orderly, appealing, and accessible to viewers.

—Lori Haller

In this chapter, you'll learn about the elements of graphic design used in logo creation, package design, and advertising. We'll take a closer look at logo creation and ad layouts in the two following chapters.

You won't become a graphic design expert overnight. You can learn enough to help your business now, either by doing your own designs or being able to provide better direction to your graphic designer.

Without knowing these design principles, your graphic designer could wreck your ads and muddle your business image. You want to sell more products and services while building your business image. You shouldn't care about winning a design award with a "creative" logo or a "fancy" advertisement. That might be the goal of your graphic designer. Also, you never want a graphic designer to start with a blank sheet of paper. You'll waste their time and your money. Instead, provide her with your avatar and target market information, your ad copy, and a concrete vision of what you're trying to accomplish. You should include sample ads from other companies, ad mockups, and your graphic design ideas.

If copywriting is more science than art, then graphic design is more art than science. Some people have an eye for color and layout, while other people are color blind. Thankfully, today's graphic design software has taken much of the design guesswork out of creating appealing websites, logos, and ads.

Your primary goal as a graphic designer is to make easy-to-read marketing materials grab attention and lead your prospect to take action.

Let's start with readability. High readability improves the results of your ads because you make it easier for the prospect to understand what you're saying. Your type font also affects the mood of your reader, because different fonts elicit different feelings.

I typeset a sentence using four different fonts. Which one is best?

A.

Readability refers to the ability of your prospect to read and understand your flyer, ad or business card.

B.

Readability refers to the ability of your prospect to read and understand your flyer, ad or business card.

C.

Readability refers to the ability of your prospect to read and understand your flyer, ad or business card.

D.

Readability refers to the ability of your prospect to read and understand your flyer, ad or business card.

I asked you a trick question. "Best type" depends on where the text is used.

For the body text of this book, "A" is the clear winner. Did you choose it? I chose 11-point Georgia with 14-point line spacing for the paperback version. Baby boomers appreciate a slightly larger font, so they might not have to grab their reading glasses. Just don't call it the large print edition. Ebook readers choose their preferred font from a short list of very readable fonts.

Choice "B" is Apple Chancery which might be used in certain target markets on a limited basis. Not in a business nonfiction book.

Choice "C" is Gil Sans in 11 point which might work for a headline font. I chose it at random from my list of hundreds of fonts.

Choice "D" is 10-point Georgia with single line spacing. This is too small and too tight to make this book easy to read. The character spacing is set at 90%. Character spacing is the space between letters.

When you learn to judge advertisements on their readability, you know one of the key fundamentals of effective graphic design.

THERE IS A REASON WHY LAWYERS USE ALL CAPS FOR THE PARTS OF CONTRACTS THEY WOULD PREFER YOU NOT READ. Most people will skim over the all-caps sections and continue reading what's easy to read. In advertisements, you need to break up large sections of copy using subheads. I do this throughout this book to guide you through each chapter.

You want your ads to be easy to read from the headline to the body copy, bullets, offer, and call to action. That's readability.

Now let's look at how to make the headline grab and keep the attention of your prospect. Take a look at this famous headline shown in four different fonts. Which one is best for headlines?

A.

**A Surprisingly Simple Way To Get "Out Of The Rat Race"
(And Into the Chips!)**

B.

A Surprisingly Simple Way To Get "Out Of The Rat Race"
(And Into the Chips!)

C.

*A Surprisingly Simple Way To Get "Out Of The Rat Race"
(And Into the Chips!)*

D.

```
A Surprisingly Simple Way To Get "Out Of The Rat
        Race" (And Into the Chips!)
```

Choice "A" is Tahoma font bold in 10 point. I used this font for example headlines in Chapter 30. This proven headline font grabs attention and is very readable. This "sans serif" font doesn't have the little curls of serif fonts such as Times Roman or the Garamond font used for choice "B".

Choice "B" is Georgia font regular in 12 point. What works well for body text, i.e., in this book, would make a poor choice for headlines.

Choice "C" is Apple Chancery bold in 12 point. Bold and frilly don't mix well. I don't like this one at all. Would your prospects?

Choice "D" is Courier bold in 10 point. Surprisingly, this "typewriter" font signals trust because it pre-dates computers. If you target an older audience, this retro font could work well for you. You would need to test "A" against "D" to know which works best.

In most markets, "A" would be the best choice for your headline. You can see how the type font dramatically changes how you perceive and feel about the headline copy.

You bring both choices of "A" together by using Tahoma for the headline and Garamond for the body copy. This contrast would make your ad or letter both readable and eye-catching.

Now I will introduce you to an amazing online graphic design tool.

Canva.com

Canva.com lets graphic design novices create excellent designs for flyers, social media images, and more and offers both free and paid versions. When I created my high school business course for the Ron Paul Curriculum, I assigned the tutorials at Canva.com. Why reinvent the wheel?

You (or an employee or spouse) can go through the tutorials at Canva.com to learn how to use Canva for flyers, ads, and a lot more. canva.com/learn/tutorials/

Canva also has many tutorials to teach you the principles of effective graphic design. canva.com/learn/design/

I'll summarize the Canva tutorials to introduce you to the elements of graphic design.

Layout. Canva defines layout as "arranging all the elements in your designs ... to create beautiful and effective compositions." Page layout means laying out the images, headline, and body copy to work together to present your marketing message.

Images. Canva lets you upload your images or use one of their free or premium images. The image should grab the attention of your prospect and draw them into your ad.

Shapes and icons. Canva includes various shapes to use in your designs. Always remember: You're want to improve your marketing communications, not win a design award.

Backgrounds. These are important when you want to create a meme for social media sharing. A meme is a background image with an overlaid headline. Be very careful that the background doesn't overwhelm the text, or the copy won't be read.

Color. Different colors evoke different feelings. Blue means trust, red means stop or passion, orange is friendly, green means grow, and so on. Some colors work well together, while other color combinations will make you gag. Be careful.

Fonts. Canva says, "Fonts bring your words to life." True, but fonts can also work against the meaning of your words. A law firm should use serious fonts, while a daycare center can use more playful fonts. Proper typography makes text easy to read and sets the tone for the chosen words. A poorly designed advertisement with too many type fonts all screaming for attention can look like a ransom note. Typology includes the type font, type size, kerning (the s p a c i n g between letters), line spacing, and type emphasis (bold, italic, or regular).

Building a Brand Kit. This process is harder than it looks but will help you if you need to design a new look and feel for your company branding or product packaging. Canva says, "Building a brand kit is the first step to create an awesome, memorable brand. Lay the foundations for your brand image by following these simple design guidelines." The three steps include choosing a color palette of four colors which represent your brand, choosing fonts for titles and subtitles, and resizing a logo.

I used Canva.com to create the cover of my book, *52 Things To Do In Southern Oregon*. I wrote this little book while creating my Ron Paul Curriculum business course. My students write a similar book about things to do in their city, state, or town. They use Canva to design the book cover for their Kindle book and then upload the cover and manuscript to Amazon.

Canva offers free and premium images for your projects. Premium images often cost only a dollar, which is a small price to pay for better exclusivity. For even better exclusivity, use original photography. For this book, I used this photograph of the Brookings, Oregon, coastline I took with my iPhone. I avoided any possibility of someone else using the same Canva image on their book cover.

Canva Design Process

Canva.com uses a simple four-step design process to create graphic images:

1. Choose a template. Canva has templates for book covers, letterhead, thank you cards, posters, social media posts, flyers, brochures, Facebook ads, business cards, and much more.

2. Change the background image. You can upload your own, choose a free image, or you can use their premium images starting at $1 each.

3. Change the text to your headline and body copy.

4. Change the color of the background, illustrations and type.

5. Click "Download" to download a PDF format for print or PNG/JPG format for online. You need higher resolution for print and lower resolution for web usage.

Graphic Design Tools

Canva.com will get you started and take you a long way. At some point, you'll want to get a graphic design software application for your computer. Here are ways to get started.

Photoshop Elements: I started with this photo editing app in 2006. Now much improved for Mac and Windows. $75 one-time purchase.

Photopea.com is a free Photoshop clone which allows you to create, edit, and save Photoshop PSD files online.

Inkscape is a free, open-source design software which creates SVG files, which stands for "scalable vector graphics." Inkscape.org

"Vector" means you can enlarge your logo to any size without pixelization. You need a vector version because you never know where your logo will appear.

Adobe Creative Cloud includes Photoshop for editing photographs, Illustrator for vector designs such as logos, and InDesign for page layout. Adobe CC has a monthly subscription price (now $53) which includes all Adobe applications. These are pro tools at a pro price with a pro learning curve.

Adobe also has a free online graphic design tool similar to Canva called Adobe Spark. https://spark.adobe.com.

I love competition because it leads to better choices for everybody. You may like Canva or prefer Spark. Either way, you can't beat the price: Free.

How To Hire a Graphic Designer

Eventually, you'll want to hire a graphic designer. You have two main places to look: local and online.

Locally, you can look at the ads and website of other small businesses in your chamber of commerce. Find out who did their graphic design work. Perhaps you can hire the same person or firm. Review their portfolios and judge their design style as suitable (or not) for your business.

Depending on what you sell, you may grow your business by developing a professional relationship with a local graphic designer. Lots of startups hire local graphic designers to help them with their logo design and branding. When you hire a local graphic designer, you may get local referrals.

If you're short on money or can't find a local graphic designer, you have other options online. Here are a few places to find freelance graphic designers.

https://www.freelancer.com/

https://www.upwork.com/cat/designers/

https://www.fiverr.com/

Either way, you must get the source files for all design work. For instance, a graphic design created in Photoshop will be saved in a lower resolution JPG or PNG format for use online. You also want the same design saved in a higher resolution PDF format for print designs. Either way, you need the Photoshop PSD file to edit the file in the future. Be prepared to pay extra for the source files. You must negotiate the amount before you pay them anything. You might part ways later and need to find a new graphic designer. Without the design source files, your designs would need to be recreated by your new graphic designer. As in so many other areas of business, "plan for the worst, hope for the best, and deal with what you get."

Finally, listen to A-list copywriter John Forde when you work with a graphic designer:

> Designers need to understand the motivations of their target market just as much as marketers and copywriters do. You or your designer must understand your marketing objectives. Don't make her work in a vacuum.

Being your own marketing consultant means you know the motivations of your clients and prospects. Tell your graphic designer about your target market and avatar so your ads will appeal to your audience.

☐ **ACTION STEP 1: Review your current ads for readability. Make notes on how to make them more readable.**

☐ **ACTION STEP 2: Open an account at Canva.com. Watch a tutorial to learn the basics of Canva. Have a little fun and create something.**

Chapter 36

Your Company Logo

> Here's a simple test: Ask a few people to name a logo they like. With very few exceptions, people will choose a logo that's associated with a brand they admire. That's because what makes a good logo is a good brand, not the other way around.
>
> —Seth Godin

You probably have little or no artistic talent and have never designed a logo. Why start now with your company logo? Far better to focus on improving your advertisements now and redesign your logo later when you can hire a professional graphic designer.

Your logo can be your company name in a distinctive font, an image only or a combination of both.

Apple Computer

Victor Schwab wrote that advertisements should not be "artsy." The same goes for your company's branding, i.e., logo. Here's a artsy logo designed in 1976 by one of the Apple Computer's co-founders, Ronald Wayne, who left the Apple Computer after only two weeks.

Yes, that's a hand-drawn image of Isaac Newton sitting under an apple tree, about to be hit by a falling apple. What an excellent example of the pitfalls of being your own graphic designer. Imagine this logo on the lid of your laptop computer, or on the back of your smartphone, tablet, or watch.

A year later Apple hired the Regis McKenna public relations agency. Their art director Rob Janoff designed Apple's logo of an apple with a bite missing. Steve Job's only direction to him was "Don't make it cute." This is good advice for you as well.

The apple-with-a-bite has served Apple well for over 40 years. You can see how Apple's logo has changed over the years.

Apple's rainbow-colored apple logo worked for 21 years. When Steve Jobs returned to the company in 1997, he had the logo redesigned to be translucent to match Apple's translucent iMac computers.

The logo's apple has a bite to avoid being seen as a cherry and to fit with the "a" in apple as shown here. Apple used the Motter Tektura font, which was also used by Reebok.

When Apple introduced the Macintosh in 1984, the apple logo stood alone without the company name. Apple also changed the corporate font to Apple Garamond. Apple used this font for 20 years before replacing it.

As Seth Godin would say, Apple's premium products and services turned the apple-with-a-bite into a premium logo. Apple's consistent logo supported over 40 years of product development. The company even changed its name, but the image provided brand continuity.

Paragon Decision Resources

I've seen the same thing happen with small companies. In 1991, I was involved in the leveraged buyout of a Weyerhaeuser subsidiary. As part of the deal, we had to change our company name by removing the word "premier" which means "best in class". Our president Joseph Morabito wanted a similar sounding business name. He went through the dictionary until he found the word "paragon," which means model of excellence and 100+ carat diamond. Our company name became Paragon Decision Resources.

Next, Joe grabbed a pencil and began doodling logo images. On flow charts, a diamond shape represents Yes/No decisions. He came up with a double diamond shape for the logo image. We chose the Trajan font for our new name. Together we had a logo for our new company.

As a leveraged buyout, we owed Weyerhaeuser $500,000, which is $931,000 in today's dollars. This money had to be paid back in five years. We had 13 employees on payroll. Money would be tight until we paid back Weyerhaeuser. Out of necessity, Joe was his own marketing consultant. Yes, we paid back the money on time and with interest. Now Paragon Global Resources assists employees and families with life decisions in over 150 countries around the world.

Joe often says, "Never change your logo," and he meant it. Here is Paragon's logo twenty-eight years later.

Very similar. Paragon Global Resources built a powerful brand and the logo image and type font remained the same. Learn more at https://paragongri.com/.

Logo Creation

Today, you can design a logo using online tools. You may find this a quick way to come up with some ideas even if you can afford to hire a graphic designer. If you're on a tight budget, you might keep this logo for years. There are many to choose from today.

I include a list of logo design tools with the book bonuses available at richardemmons.com/marketingbonus.

Let me show you the results of two of these tools.

I used logaster.com to create a logo for richardemmons.com. You can buy the logo for $10-25 depending on resolution. The $25 version includes the vector format (SVG) which can be edited in Photoshop or Illustrator. Here is the free preview version which is low resolution. Not too shabby for ten minutes of work.

I created this logo at Canva.com in about 5 minutes. That includes the time to create the slogan. https://www.canva.com/create/logos/

I could give either of these logos to my graphic designer and let her take it from there. Or I could use one of them and get back to business.

Logo Examples

Here are a few well-known logos. One has a graphic image. All use a distinctive font in their logo.

Forbes

Forbes magazine has changed its logo numerous times over the past 100 years. It has remained the same since 1999.

FedEx®

The FedEx logo includes a hidden arrow between the capital E and the x. The arrow stands for speed and precision. Do you see it?

amazon

The Amazon logo has an orange arrow with a dual purpose. Amazon sells everything from a to z, and it forms a smile. Now you know.

Yes, Amazon.com changed its original logo, too. Here's the Amazon logo scanned from the packing slip of the first book sold in July 1995.

amazon.com

Wow. What a dated logo. That was from the days when Amazon referred to a river in South America. No wonder they changed it.

These days your logo should look great on a baseball cap, product packaging, and your website. Simpler is better. Make it easy to read and avoid complicated graphical elements. Learn from the logos of successful companies. Hire a professional graphic designer. Tell her "don't make it cute." And resist changing your logo later.

ACTION STEP: Do you have a logo? Does it need help? Don't have a logo? A better logo should not be your top priority now. Keep reading.

Chapter 37

Graphic Design for Display Ads

Fancy design isn't always good design. Your first aim is
readability. Your second is to make sure the copy isn't
obscured by the design. Good design makes the copy
look and feel easy to read.

—John Forde

Display ads can be placed in magazines, newspapers, yellow pages,
billboards, and online. You get one chance to make a good first
impression, so your graphic design will make or break the success of
your display advertisement.

When you create a display ad, be sure to create the copy first and
then work on graphic design. You'll save money and aggravation.

One time, my client Dave asked me to place a display ad in our
local newspaper. He told me to set up a meeting with our graphic
designer. I pointed out we first need to create the "copy" or message
for the ad. Dave got a little impatient and asked, "Why can't we just
do that with the graphic designer?" Seeing that the "customer is
always right," I replied, "No problem. I'll create the headline, body,
offer, and call to action while the graphic designer sits there at $65 per
hour." That got us back on track.

After I write the ad copy rough draft, I format it into an ad mockup
using Microsoft Word. I begin editing the ad copy to fit the available
space. I tighten the ad copy by eliminating wordiness and making the
ad more persuasive. A mockup gives the client an idea of how the
advertisement will look. A mockup also gives the graphic designer a
place to start based on the client's and copywriter's thoughts.

Now the graphic designer can get to work. Her job is to help the
copy stand out and get read.

In *How to Write a Good Advertisement*, Victor Schwab offers two ways to use the ad layout to get attention.

1. Make it so powerful, so unusual, or so dynamically dominating that it captures the eye despite the competition of other advertisements less unique or less positive in their impact.

2. Or you may make your layout so uncommonly simple, sedate, or "nonprofessional" that its very restraint captures attention.

Of course, either the first or the second type of layout is extreme; but the more "neutral" your layout, the more likely it is to be passed by.

Victor Schwab also offers ways to use pictures to increase attention.

1. Large, simple photographs of people, children, and animals get more attention.

2. Having a picture of your product IN USE—doing something or accomplishing something that appeals to the reader—is more likely to get attention.

The Advertorial Format

Author and copywriter Ted Nicholas spent hundreds of millions of dollars on full-page magazine display ads. He used these ads to sell over a billion dollars' worth of books and information products. He tested every configuration imaginable to see what worked best. The winner? Usually, the "advertorial" format worked best: An advertorial is an ad which looks like an editorial. On some products, a picture helped. He tested small and rolled out big.

Depending on the ad placement, the ad could be black and white, two-color, or full color. A picture which supports the message is helpful. A picture of you will personalize the ad, especially if you are the service provider. You can use a picture of a worried person to evoke an emotional response.

In *Billion Dollar Marketing Secrets*, Ted Nicholas wrote, "Never run a photo, even if it's you, without a caption, assuming the reader will figure it out. Many won't. Always include a caption describing the subject of the picture." Don't make people guess about anything in your ads. Caption the photograph so they keep reading the ad copy rather than slowing down to figure out the picture.

Now we'll look at two magazine advertisements created by Ted Nicholas. He used these ads successfully in 1978 and 1979 in such publications as *The Wall Street Journal, Fortune, Business Week,* and *The New York Times.* The ads contain every element we've covered in earlier chapters, including an attention-grabbing headline, a strong lead to draw in the reader, lots of benefits, testimonials, a strong guarantee, how to buy, and a coupon keycode to track which advertisement made the sale.

Yes, the font is too small to read in a book. I'll include this ad with the book bonuses. You will learn more about effective copywriting and graphic design by studying successful classic ads like this one.

In the next ad, Ted Nicholas advertises the same book in a different publication. Notice the easy readability with a curiosity headline, subheads to guide the reader, left-justified body copy, and a clear call to action at the end. Ted Nicholas brings it all together for a brilliant and profitable ad. Ted Nicholas included a copyright notice so competitors couldn't copy his ads.

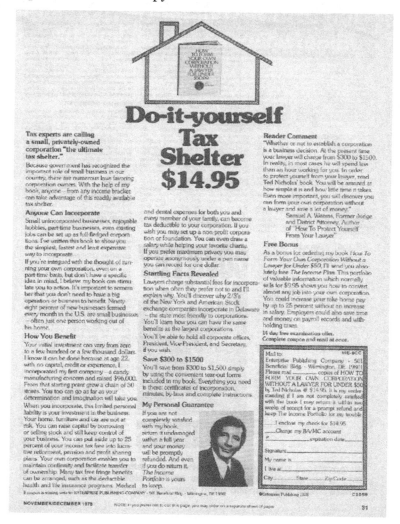

When you want to advertise in a magazine or newspaper, study the graphic design of the publication and try to blend in your ad as an article.

Here is an advertorial created by David Ogilvy of Ogilvy and Mather, one of the top advertising agencies of the 20th century. Ogilvy created this advertisement for his agency at a time when most advertising agencies used image advertising. The headline makes a big promise. The rest of the ad offers proof to back up the headline. For people like you and me who depend on advertising to pay the bills, we would have read this ad.

How to create advertising that sells

by David Ogilvy

Ogilvy & Mather has created over $1,480,000,000 worth of advertising, and spent $4,900,000 tracking the results.

Here, with all the dogmatism of brevity, are 38 of the things we have learned.

1. The most important decision. We have learned that the effect of your advertising on your sales depends more on this decision than on any other: *How should you position your product?*

Should you position SCHWEPPES as a soft drink—or as a mixer?

Should you position DOVE as a product for dry skin or as a product which gets hands really clean?

The results of your campaign depend less on how we write your advertising than on how your product is positioned. It follows that positioning should be decided before the advertising is created.

Research can help. Look before you leap.

2. Large promise. The second most important decision is this: what should you promise the customer? A promise is not a claim, or a theme, or a slogan. It is a *benefit for the consumer.*

It pays to promise a benefit which is unique and competitive. And the product must *deliver* the benefit you promise.

Most advertising promises *nothing.* It is doomed to fail in the marketplace.

"Promise, large promise, is the soul of an advertisement"—said Samuel Johnson.

3. Brand image. Every advertisement should contribute to the complex symbol which is the brand image. Ninety-five percent of all advertising is created *ad hoc.* Most products lack any consistent image from one year to another.

The manufacturer who dedicates his advertising to building the most sharply defined personality for his brand gets the largest share of the market.

4. Big ideas. Unless your advertising is built on a BIG IDEA it will pass like a ship in the night.

It takes a BIG IDEA to jolt the consumer out of his indifference—to make him *notice* your advertising, *remember* it and *take action.*

Big ideas are usually *simple* ideas. Said Charles Kettering, the great General Motors inventor: "This problem, when solved, will be simple."

BIG SIMPLE IDEAS are not easy to come by. They require genius—and midnight oil. A truly big one can be continued for twenty years—like our Eyepatch for Hathaway shirts.

5. A first-class ticket. It pays to give most products an image of quality—a first-class ticket.

Ogilvy & Mather has been conspicuously successful in doing this—for Pepperidge, Hathaway, Mercedes-Benz, Schweppes, Dove and others.

If your advertising looks ugly, consumers will conclude that your product is shoddy, and they will be less likely to buy it.

6. Don't be a bore. Nobody was ever *bored* into buying a product. Yet most advertising is impersonal, detached, cold—and dull.

It pays to *involve* the customer.

Talk to her like a human being. Charm her. Make her hungry. Get her to participate.

7. Innovate. Start trends—instead of following them. Advertising which follows a fashionable fad, or is imitative, is seldom successful.

It pays to *innovate,* to blaze new trails.

But innovation is risky unless you pretest your innovation with consumers. Look before you leap.

8. Be suspicious of awards. The pursuit of creative awards seduces creative people from the pursuit of sales.

We have been unable to establish any correlation whatever between awards and sales.

At Ogilvy & Mather we now give an annual award for the campaign which contributes the most to *sales.*

Successful advertising sells the product without drawing attention to itself. It rivets the consumer's attention on the *product.*

Make the product the hero of your advertising.

9. Psychological segmentation. Any good agency knows how to position products for *demographic* segments of the market—for men, for young children, for farmers in the South, etc.

But Ogilvy & Mather has learned that it often pays to position products for *psychological* segments of the market.

Our Mercedes-Benz advertising is positioned to fit nonconformists who scoff at "status symbols" and reject flimflam appeals to snobbery.

10. Don't bury news. It is easier to interest the consumer in a product when it is *new* than at any other point in its life. Many copywriters have a fatal instinct for burying news. This is why most advertising for new products fails to exploit the opportunity that genuine news provides.

It pays to launch your new product with a loud BOOM-BOOM.

11. Go the whole hog. Most advertising campaigns are too complicated. They reflect a long list of marketing objectives. They embrace the divergent views of too many executives. By attempting too many things, they achieve nothing.

It pays to boil down your strategy to one simple promise—and go the whole hog in delivering that promise.

What works best in television

12. Testimonials: Avoid irrelevant celebrities. Testimonial commercials are almost always successful—if you make them credible.

Either celebrities or real people can be effective. But avoid *irrelevant* celebrities whose fame has no natural connection with your product or your customers. Irrelevant celebrities steal attention from your product.

13. Problem-solution (don't cheat!) You set up a problem that the consumer recognizes.

Then you show how your product can solve that problem.

And you prove the solution.

This technique has always been above average in sales results, and it still is. But don't use it unless you can do so *without cheating;* the consumer isn't a moron, she is your wife.

14. Visual demonstrations. If they are honest, visual demonstrations are generally effective in the marketplace.

It pays to *visualize your promise.* It saves time. It drives the promise home. It is memorable.

15. Slice of life. These playlets are corny, and most copywriters detest them. But they have sold a lot of merchandise, and are still selling.

16. Avoid logorrhea. Make your *pictures* tell the story. What you *show* is more important than what you say.

Many commercials drown the viewer in a torrent of words. We call that logorrhea (rhymes with diarrhea).

We have created some great commercials *without* words.

17. On-camera voice. Commercials using on-camera voice do significantly better than commercials using voice-over.

18. Musical backgrounds. Most commercials use musical backgrounds. However, on the average, musical backgrounds reduce recall of your commercial. Very few creative people accept this. But we never heard of an agency using musical background under a new business presentation.

19. Stand-ups. The stand-up pitch can be effective, if it is delivered with straightforward honesty.

20. Burr of singularity. The average consumer now sees 20,000 commercials a year; poor dear.

Most of them slide off her memory like water off a duck's back.

Give your commercials a flourish of singularity, a burr that will stick in the consumer's mind. One such burr is the MNEMONIC DEVICE, or relevant symbol—like the crowns in our commercials for Imperial Margarine.

21. Animation & cartoons. Less than five percent of television commercials use cartoons or animation. They are less persuasive than live commercials.

The consumer cannot identify herself with the character in the cartoon. And cartoons do not invite belief.

However, Carson/Roberts, our partners in Los Angeles, tell us that animation can be helpful when you are talking to children.

They should know—they have addressed more than six hundred commercials to children.

22. Salvage commercials. Many commercials which test poorly can be salvaged.

The faults revealed by the test can be corrected. We have *doubled* the effectiveness of a commercial simply by re-editing it.

23. Factual vs. emotional. Factual commercials tend to be more effective than emotional commercials.

However, Ogilvy & Mather has made some emotional commercials which have been successful in the marketplace. Among these are our campaigns for Maxwell House Coffee and Hershey's Milk Chocolate.

24. Grabbers. We have found that commercials with an exciting opening hold their audience at a higher level than commercials which begin quietly.

What works best in print

25. Headlines. On the average, five times as many people read the headline as read the body copy.

It follows that, if you don't sell the product in your headline, you have wasted 80 percent of your money. That is why most Ogilvy & Mather headlines include the brand name and the promise.

26. Benefit in headlines. Headlines that promise a benefit sell more than those that don't.

27. News in headlines. Time after time, we have found that it pays to inject genuine news into headlines.

The consumer is always on the lookout for new products, or new improvements in an old product, or new ways to use an old product.

Economists—even Russian economists—approve of this. They call it "informative" advertising. So do consumers.

28. Simple headlines. Your headline should *telegraph* what you want to say—in simple language. Readers do not stop to decipher the meaning of obscure headlines.

29. How many words in a headline? In headline tests conducted with the cooperation of a big department store, it was found that headlines of ten words or longer sold more goods than short headlines.

In terms of *recall,* headlines between eight and ten words are most effective.

In *mail-order* advertising, headlines between six and twelve words get the most coupon returns.

On the average, long headlines sell more merchandise than short ones—headlines like our "At 60 miles an hour, the loudest noise in this new Rolls-Royce comes from the electric clock."

30. Localize headlines. In local advertising it pays to include the name of the city in your headline.

31. Select your prospects. When you advertise a product which is consumed only by a special group, it pays to "flag" that group in your headline—MOTHERS, BED-WETTERS, GOING TO EUROPE?

32. Yes, people read long copy. Readership falls off rapidly up to fifty words, but drops very little between fifty and five hundred words. (This page contains 1909 words, and you are reading it.)

Ogilvy & Mather has used long copy—with notable success—for Mercedes-Benz, Cessna Citation, Merrill Lynch and Shell gasoline.

"The more you tell, the more you sell."

33. Story appeal in picture. Ogilvy & Mather has gotten notable results with photographs which suggest a story. The reader glances at the photograph and asks himself, "What goes on here?" Then he reads the copy to find out.

Harold Rudolph called this magic element "story appeal." The more of it you inject into your photograph, the more people look at your advertisement.

It is easier said than done.

34. Before & after. Before and After advertisements are somewhat above average in attention value.

Any form of "visualized contrast" seems to work well.

35. Photographs vs. artwork. Ogilvy & Mather has found that photographs work better than drawings—almost invariably.

They attract more readers, generate more appetite appeal, are more believable, are better remembered, pull more coupons, and sell more merchandise.

36. Use captions to sell. On the average, twice as many people read the captions under photographs as read the body copy.

It follows that you should never use a photograph without putting a caption under it; and each caption should be a miniature advertisement for the product—complete with brand name and promise.

37. Editorial layouts. Ogilvy & Mather has had more success with editorial layouts than with "addy" layouts.

Editorial layouts get higher readership than conventional advertisements.

38. Repeat your winners. Scores of great advertisements have been discarded before they have begun to pay off.

Readership can actually *increase* with repetition—up to five repetitions.

Is this all we know?

These findings apply to most categories of products. But not to all.

Ogilvy & Mather has developed a separate and specialized body of knowledge on what makes for success in advertising *food products, tourist destinations, proprietary medicines, children's products*—and other classifications.

But this special information is revealed only to the clients of Ogilvy & Mather.

Ogilvy & Mather

2 East 48th Street, New York, N.Y. 10017

David Ogilvy's Classic Magazine Layout

Ogilvy & Mather's most famous ad was created for Rolls-Royce. The ad layout had five main elements: Image, caption, headline, copy, and call to action. Often the CTA was a coupon. In this case, the opposing page in the magazine had dealer phone numbers and addresses. Yes, back then you could buy a Rolls-Royce for under $14,000.

The Rolls-Royce Silver Cloud—$13,995

"At 60 miles an hour the loudest noise in this new Rolls-Royce comes from the electric clock"

What makes Rolls-Royce the best car in the world? "There is really no magic about it— it is merely patient attention to detail," says an eminent Rolls-Royce engineer.

1. "At 60 miles an hour the loudest noise comes from the electric clock," reports the Technical Editor of THE MOTOR. Three mufflers tune out sound frequencies—acoustically.

2. Every Rolls-Royce engine is run for seven hours at full throttle before installation, and each car is test-driven for hundreds of miles over varying road surfaces.

3. The Rolls-Royce is designed as an owner-driven car. It is eighteen inches shorter than the largest domestic cars.

4. The car has power steering, power brakes and automatic gear-shift. It is very easy to drive and to park. No chauffeur required.

5. The finished car spends a week in the final test-shop, being fine-tuned. Here it is subjected to 98 separate ordeals. For example, the engineers use a *stethoscope* to listen for axle-whine.

6. The Rolls-Royce is guaranteed for *three* years. With a new network of dealers and parts-depots from Coast to Coast, service is no problem.

7. The Rolls-Royce radiator has never changed, except that when Sir Henry Royce died in 1933 the monogram RR was changed from red to black.

8. The coachwork is given five coats of primer paint, and hand rubbed between each coat, before nine coats of finishing paint go on.

9. By moving a switch on the steering column, you can adjust the shock-absorbers to suit road conditions.

10. A picnic table, veneered in French walnut, slides out from under the dash. Two more swing out behind the front seats.

11. You can get such optional extras as an Espresso coffee-making machine, a dictating machine, a bed, hot and cold water for washing, an electric razor or a telephone.

12. There are three separate systems of power brakes, two hydraulic and one mechanical. Damage to one system will not affect the others. The Rolls-Royce is a very safe car—and also a very lively car. It cruises serenely at eighty-five. Top speed is in excess of 100 m.p.h.

13. The Bentley is made by Rolls-Royce. Except for the radiators, they are identical motor cars, manufactured by the same engineers in the same works. People who feel diffident about driving a Rolls-Royce can buy a Bentley.

PRICE. The Rolls-Royce illustrated in this advertisement—f.o.b. principal ports of entry—costs **$13,995.**

If you would like the rewarding experience of driving a Rolls-Royce or Bentley, write or telephone to one of the dealers listed on the opposite page.

Rolls-Royce Inc., 10 Rockefeller Plaza, New York 20, N. Y., Circle 5-1144.

March 1959

Common Graphic Design Mistakes

Beware of graphic designers who want to really jazz up your ads. Tell them you want to win new clients. Not win a design award.

For instance, you should avoid using white text on a black background. If this effect made headlines more readable, wouldn't newspapers do it this way? Newspapers don't and neither should you.

Which of these headlines pops out as an advertisement?

Free Community Seminar Offers Tips for New Home Buyers

Free Community Seminar Offers Tips for New Home Buyers

Don't just take my word for this. Listen to A-list copywriter John Forde who wrote about this in his article, "Graphic Design: The Look That Sells."

> Graphics and design are a vital part of any sales letter. But before you let your graphic designer take over, make sure you keep this in mind:

> Always, always, always ask your designer to read the copy. I'm blown away by how many don't. And it shows. Boy, does it show.

> The general rule is that good design can't make bad copy work, but bad design can destroy the performance of good copy.

> If you throw your finished sales piece onto a table with other finished sales pieces ... and it disappears into the pile ... you've got a problem.

> No screened images behind text. No screened images behind text. Did I mention? Please avoid screened images behind text.

> When in doubt, cut graphics before cutting copy. Really. By the time the designer gets a piece, the copy should be airtight. Or close to it. Graphics are less important than the written message. That's just the way it goes.

Follow these guidelines, and the design of your sales pieces will always enhance – not detract from – your sales message.

For more great copywriting ideas, you should subscribe to John Forde's free e-newsletter, "The Copywriter's Roundtable," at his site, copywritersroundtable.com.

Over the years, I've gotten into tug-of-wars with graphic designers.

"Too many words!" they complain.

I respond, "How do you know? If the reader is interested in the product or service, they'll read everything they can about it!"

"It's boring!"

"So what? It sells product!" And so on.

Of course, if you have money to burn you can test two versions against each other and see if glitz beats informative and persuasive copy. Let the market decide.

You can learn how to create winning ads for your business by studying winning ads from the past. Why? Because human nature has not changed. I include a collection of classic ads with the book bonuses available at richardemmons.com/marketingbonus.

> ☐ **ACTION STEP: Review the graphic design of your ads. Does the layout and typology of your ads draw a prospect in and make him want to read more? Does the graphic design enhance or obscure the ad copy?**

Chapter 38

Get Started With Online Advertising

> It was the best of times, it was the worst of times, it was
> the age of wisdom, it was the age of foolishness, it was
> the epoch of belief, it was the epoch of incredulity, it was
> the season of Light, it was the season of Darkness, it was
> the spring of hope, it was the winter of despair, we had
> everything before us, we had nothing before us, we were
> all going direct to Heaven, we were all going direct the
> other way ...
>
> —Charles Dickens, *A Tale of Two Cities*

Charles Dickens could have been speaking about online advertising in 2019. When done correctly, advertising on Google and Facebook can be the best of times because you can target your avatar with extreme precision. Online advertising is also an age of foolishness because you can spend a lot of money quickly and end up with little or no results.

Your experience may cause you to believe it is the greatest thing ever or be incredibly skeptical because you spent money and got nothing back. Or you may be baffled by it all rather than filled with hope or despair.

You can advertise online successfully if you've followed the path of the first 37 chapters. Why is this? Most businesses fail in their online advertising campaigns because they don't have a proven offer to a clearly defined market. You have your avatar and understand your target market.

Many businesses target the right audience but don't use a compelling headline. You have your USP which makes a great headline and is unique in your local area. You also know other ways to create great headlines.

Other businesses may know whom to target and have a compelling headline, offer, and call to action. Yet they send their "clicks" to their home page. Why is this a bad idea? Because these prospects get confronted with a different headline, different offers, lots of articles, lots of products and services, and information about your company's history. All of this information is nice, but it takes the focus off the objective of the online advertisement. The prospect may click the ad but never make a purchase.

How do you overcome this? You create a custom landing page for your online ads. The prospect clicks the ad which takes him to your landing page.

For example, let's say I want to promote this book on Facebook. I run a Facebook ad with the book cover and a promise to help brick-and-mortar business owners escape the rat race. When the owner clicks through, I do not want them to land on richardemmons.com. There is too much information, most of which does not keep the focus on their problem and my book.

Instead, I direct them to a landing page which tells them all about this book, i.e., richardemmons.com/marketing. At the bottom of this landing page, I offer ways to take action, i.e., buy the book.

I can create three different Facebook ads and test them against each other. After a short test, Facebook displays the best ad based on the number of clicks for each of the three ads. Once I know the ad is working, I can increase my ad budget and get in front of more likely buyers.

I can also promote the book using Google Ads, which used to be branded as Google AdWords. On this platform, I pay for clicks from people who enter specific keywords into the Google search engine. In my case, this could be "local business marketing" or "marketing consulting."

You can do the same thing for your products and services.

I get it that Facebook knows far too much about you, me, our families, and our friends. The flip side of the loss of privacy is that Facebook knows all about your target prospects and will sell you ads to reach them. We're in business to help people live better lives with our products and services. Facebook, Google Ads, YouTube, and other online advertisers now make it very easy to reach them.

Becoming your own marketing consultant requires that you make marketing one of your core competencies. You should never entirely delegate marketing to an employee or marketing firm. You must remain in charge, set goals, and approve budgets. However, doing online advertising yourself could put you in the fast lane to wasting time and money. Online advertising is a fast-moving target. What works great now may not work well later.

You can start out small and spend a little money on your own. When you are spending $5,000 a month or more, you better pay someone else to manage the day-to-day process and create the ads. Your online advertising can and should pay for itself, but it takes ongoing attention to keep it working.

How should you get started? Choose one platform and learn how to use it well. This work can be done by you, an employee, or an outside firm.

If you have a Facebook page and lots of likes, start with Facebook. Facebook ads will feed your ads to people similar to people who have already "liked" your Facebook page.

Google Ads

Google Ads is PPC ("pay per click") advertising with prices set by bids in an auction setting. You will pay an enormous amount per click for popular keywords. At the moment, "life insurance" will set you back between $17.58 and $38.71 for one click. You pay when someone clicks and not when someone takes out a life insurance policy and you earn a commission. PPC gets expensive quickly. You better have a great offer.

Google Ads bid prices have risen sharply as more businesses show up for the auction. It's all about supply and demand, and businesses with deeper pockets bid more so keywords cost more. However, you can limit who sees your ads to people in your local area only. These clicks usually cost less than trying to get clicks on a national basis.

Google Ads can be used to test headlines and offers. You create ads with different headlines and the same offer. Or you use the same headline with different offers. You can start with a minimal budget, i.e., $5 per day, to test one ad against another, and have test results in a week or even less. These tests help you determine which headline to use in a more expensive advertising medium such as a magazine ad.

Facebook Ads

Greater demand for online advertising also raised ad prices at Facebook. AdStage is a Facebook advertising agency. They analyzed over 8.8 billion Facebook ad impressions in 2017: "We found that during the first six months [of 2017], the average CPM increased from $4.12 to $11.17, and the average CPC increased from $0.42 to $0.99."

CPM stands for "cost per thousand impressions" which means someone saw your ad. CPC stands for "cost per click" which means someone saw your ad and clicked it. CTR stands for "click-through rate" which is the percentage of ad viewers who clicked on an ad. CTR was 2.38% as of March 2018.

There is only so much room for more ads on Facebook. Yet the number of Facebook advertisers is skyrocketing. AdStage reported there were 5 million advertisers on Facebook out of 65 million businesses on Facebook. This was up from 3 million the year before. This huge increase in advertisers with limited room for more ads means higher CPM and CPC.

I strongly urge you to implement the marketing fundamentals taught in this book before making online advertising a priority in your business. Your business can benefit from a strong USP for ten years. One of your competitors can copy a well-crafted and profitable Facebook ad in ten minutes.

> **ACTION STEP: Do you currently advertise online? If so, improve your ads with better headlines and offers. If not, work on improving your offline advertising now and focus on online advertising later.**

Chapter 39

Where Should I Advertise?

Go where the money is ... and go there often.
—Willy Sutton, American bank robber

Advertising can be a great way to get more prospects in the door. You should advertise in those advertising mediums which cost-effectively deliver your message to your desired market. In short, you advertise somewhere because that's where the money is for your business.

I am not suggesting that effective advertising is equivalent to bank robbery. However, you should remember Willy Sutton's famous line. You should advertise in those places where your targeted clientele reads, watches, or listens. For example, a financial planner shouldn't advertise in a financial planning magazine because that's what his competitors read. Instead, the financial planner might advertise in a local square-dancing newsletter because active retirees often enjoy square dancing. If you're going after local businesses, consider advertising in your local chamber of commerce newsletter.

You can ask your best clients what magazines they like to read, what TV shows they watch, and how often they use the Yellow Pages. Don't be shocked if they answer, "Yellow pages? I Google everything!" You might be shocked to learn that they still read the Yellow Pages. You won't know until you ask. The most direct way is to ask your clients at the end of meetings. In a retail environment, you can ask customers at checkout to complete a quick questionnaire.

These informal survey results can eliminate a lot of waste from your advertising budget—and help you determine how much you should advertise in newspapers, magazines, radio, and yellow pages versus online advertising. Knowing where to advertise is a moving target, so try to stay in touch with your best clients for clues on where to advertise.

We covered how to use key codes, coupons, and landing pages to track ad performance in Chapter 33. Key coding lets you know what's working, because a specific ad brought specific leads into your business. Is this too complicated for you now? Then you and your employees can simply ask every new prospect, "How did you find out about us?" You must know what ads are working and what's not working.

In the old days, it was common for a city to have three or four different Yellow Pages directories. Businesses would typically run the same ad with the same phone number in every directory. You had no way to know which directory was helping you. Now you can use a different phone number for each directory. After a year, you'll know the best source of phone call leads. You can cancel the other directories at renewal time without losing any sleep.

80/20 Tip: Surveys and lead tracking let you advertise to your 20% Clients based on proven messages on proven advertising platforms. You know what's working for your business. You advertise scientifically instead on a whim. You'll laugh in the face of advertising reps who knock on your door and say, "Hey I'm selling space on a billboard. Would you like to advertise your business?" That's not the right way to choose where to advertise.

What does a new restaurant need more than anything else to be a successful restaurant? Hungry people! Restaurants should advertise where and when hungry people are likely to hang out.

This holds true for every type of business: Know your market and its problems and wants. Hunt for hungry prospects. Then put an effective advertisement in front of them.

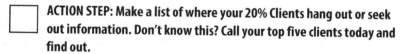

ACTION STEP: Make a list of where your 20% Clients hang out or seek out information. Don't know this? Call your top five clients today and find out.

Note: When I mapped out this book, I included a fifth section called, "Advertising From A to Z." As I wrote this book that section grew to more than 100 pages. Would this book get too big to be readable? Would I ever get it done?

At a Toastmasters meeting, I asked Audrey and Evan what they thought about this. "Second book!" they said in unison. That was it.

This decision turned out for the best for another big reason. *Marketing Survival Guide* is about using proven marketing strategies to maximize your current advertising programs. The next volume in the Local Business Success Series will help you choose additional advertising mediums to test out and find new prospects.

Tackle this book first, and my next book will amplify what you learn here.

Chapter 40

Set Your Advertising Budget

Advertising is like vitamins. A little is good and more is better.

—Advertising salesperson

Truth in advertising disclosure: I made up that quote based on a true story. Many true stories. I'm speaking as a recovering ad salesperson.

Now back to your advertising budget. Many business books and blog posts recommend spending 5 or 10% of your gross sales on advertising. This general rule is better than nothing, because few businesses can budget zero for advertising and have a growing and successful business. However, this simple rule of thumb is more wrong than right. Here's why:

- A flat percentage of sales does not differentiate between advertising to cold prospects and advertising to your best clients.

- Spending "10% of sales" does not differentiate between image advertising and direct response advertising. I recommend spending most or all of your advertising on direct response advertising because you need to measure the results of your ads.

- Image advertising is a form of gambling for small businesses. You don't know if you're winning or losing. At least with slot machines, you know immediately.

- Advertising agencies prefer image advertising because they can't be held accountable for a failed advertising campaign. Plus, ad agencies usually get paid a percentage of your advertising expenditures. The more you spend on advertising, the more you pay your advertising agency.

- You can test a direct response ad with a small ad budget and roll it out big after you know you have a winner. This has nothing to do with "5 or 10% of sales."

A better question is, "How much can I spend to get a new client?" We cover "Lifetime Value of Clients" in Chapter 44. This calculation gives you the answer to this question. Here's the short version.

Would you spend a dollar to get a new client who generates a dollar profit on their first purchase? You would if you knew this client would generate another $5 in profit over the rest of the year and for the next five years. You would want to spend more on advertising because each dollar spent pays for itself and creates a mini-annuity for your business.

With proven direct response ads, the more you spend, the more you make. If you underspend on advertising, you'll be riding the brake on your company's growth. You view advertising as an investment which pays you back with new clients.

You don't have to spend any money on traditional advertising when you use endorsement letters, referral systems, and networking strategies to gain new clients. You "advertise" to your clients with direct mail, in-store specials, and invitation-only events. You help your clients get more of what they want. You stop spending money on newspaper, magazine, TV, radio, billboards, and online advertising.

Your competitors will wonder how you stay in business because you "never" advertise. Your secret is safe with me.

☐ **ACTION STEP: Review where you've spent advertising dollars over the past three years. Calculate dollars spent annually for advertising platforms such as Yellow Pages, Facebook, radio, and magazines. You may need to ask your CPA or bookkeeper about this. Can you point to any specific sales from your advertising? Can you identify any advertising spending which is a total waste? Plan to either improve it so it works or just eliminate it.**

Review of Part 3

Marketing is simply helping your intended
market/audience discover you.

—Jay Abraham

You now know many proven ways to get noticed in your marketplace
by prospects who want to buy what you have for sell.

First, you can get noticed without spending money on advertising.
You do this by getting involved in your local chamber of commerce.
You join other business networking groups. You serve your
community by volunteering at a local non-profit organization. You
join a Toastmasters club and give speeches about your business
services. As people get to know you and your business, they buy your
products and services. People also refer you to friends and family
members who need what you offer.

Next, we looked at using endorsement letters to get quality new
clients by spending a little money on letterhead and postage.
Depending on your industry, endorsement letters could be the most
powerful marketing technique taught in this book.

You learned the basics of copywriting and how to structure and
write effective advertisements. If you're spending a lot of money on
advertising, you can use these copywriting techniques to increase the
effectiveness of your ads dramatically. You'll increase your profits
because your ads will bring more clients for the same amount of
money. Start by improving your headlines.

You learned the basics of graphic design for advertisements and
where to go to get online tools and training.

Finally, you learned why and when to get started with online
advertising and how to choose where to advertise your business.

I'll summarize each chapter of Part 3 into a single sentence:

Chapter 20: You can get noticed by spending time rather than
money on advertising.

Chapter 21: You can get quality clients quickly by mailing

endorsement letters to a noncompetitor's client list.

Chapter 22: An effective advertisement is one which makes a sale.

Chapter 23: Can you afford image advertising? No.

Chapter 24: Direct response advertising gets you clients and builds your image.

Chapter 25: You know the easiest way to improve any advertisement.

Chapter 26: Know the process to create an effective ad campaign.

Chapter 27: Your avatar is your A-list client personified.

Chapter 28: Use these seven copywriting techniques to improve your ads.

Chapter 29: No reason to create a new advertisement with a blank sheet of paper.

Chapter 30: Your headline grabs the attention of your target prospect.

Chapter 31: Your offer says what your prospect gets for his money and the terms.

Chapter 32: Your call to action persuades your prospect to do something now.

Chapter 33: You should care which ad brings in every prospect to your business.

Chapter 34: How to review your ad copy before the graphic design work begins.

Chapter 35: Your graphic design crash course to make you more than dangerous.

Chapter 36: Your company logo helps define your brand.

Chapter 37: Using graphic design to help your ad copy sell.

Chapter 38: How and when to get started with online advertising.

Chapter 39: Where to advertise your business and why.

Chapter 40: Advertising is an investment to get long-lasting targeted clients.

In Part 4 you will learn how to get and stay connected with your existing clients. As you increase your sales to existing clients, you can stop chasing down cold prospects and getting that first sale. You can reduce your advertising budget. You'll also learn how to reactivate past clients–which is easier than it sounds.

Part 4: Stay Connected

"Sometimes you have to treat
them like a *dysfunctional* family."

Introduction to Part 4

I want to be better at staying connected.
—Benedict Cumberbatch

You've learned why you must make marketing a core competency in your business. You know why you must set your business apart from your competitors with a USP. You know why effective advertising leads directly to sales. You improved your advertising and now have new clients to serve. Now in Part 4, we'll look at ways to stay in touch with your clients.

Why stay in touch with your clients?

First, you want to sell them more products and services.

Second, your clients must feel that you care about them. I assume that you do. Bad things happen when clients don't feel it: You lose them.

In 2008, John Gattorna, a visiting professor at Macquarie Graduate School of Management, published the following figures on why businesses lose customers:

4% Natural attrition (e.g., moved away, passed on, etc.)

5% Referred to a competitor by their friend

9% Competitive reasons (e.g., price)

14% Product/service dissatisfaction

68% Perceived indifference

(Source: retrieved on 1/7/2019 customerthermometer.com/customer-satisfaction/csat-stat-68-percent/)

Only 9% of customers left due to competitive reasons such as a lower price. Just 14% of customers left because they were dissatisfied with the product or service. Amazingly, 68% of customers left due to "perceived indifference." This means five times as many customers leave for feeling neglected as leave for product or service dissatisfaction. You must market to your clients, or they will feel neglected and look elsewhere. That means your competitors.

Should you improve your products and services? Of course, but how does a better product or service help a client who left your business? It doesn't. Demonstrate that you care about your clients by staying in touch with them, and you will keep them for the long haul. You won't need to add as many new clients when you reduce client losses, i.e., increase client retention.

Client retention math is simple. If a company adds 20% new clients each year yet loses 20% of existing clients, they will work very hard, spend a lot of money on advertising, and have zero growth. We'll look at this closely in Chapter 45.

Thankfully, today we have more ways to stay in touch than ever before. Here are the topics we'll cover in Part 4:

Chapter 41: Serve Your Clients

Chapter 42: Know Your Clients

Chapter 43: Client Referral Systems

Chapter 44: Lifetime Value of Clients

Chapter 45: Reconnect with Past Clients

Chapter 46: Your Website, Your Platform

Chapter 47: Does Your Website Need a Makeover?

Chapter 48: Create Your Marketing Planner

Chapter 49: Greeting Cards

Chapter 50: Emails Are Sales Letters

Chapter 51: Email Marketing

Chapter 52: Print Newsletters

Chapter 53: Client Letters Are Sales Letters

Chapter 54: Client Appreciation Dinners

Chapter 55: Client Meetings

Chapter 41

Serve Your Clients

People are silently begging to be acknowledged,
informed, given advance opportunities and led to action.

—Jay Abraham

Let's dissect Jay Abraham's insightful words to learn how you can use his wisdom to grow your business by treating your clients well. We'll also learn how you mistreat your clients by not practicing this in your business. There are four parts to Jay's words of wisdom here:

1. Acknowledge your clients.

2. Inform your clients.

3. Give your clients special deals.

4. Lead your clients to take action.

First, acknowledge your clients. The norm in business is to constantly focus on getting new clients while ignoring existing clients. No one wants to feel neglected. This is as true in business relationships as it is in personal relationships. I remember spending $16,000 on a 15-passenger van. This van was a huge purchase for our family. We needed it when our four daughters started a bluegrass band. Did I ever hear back from the car salesperson after the sale? No. The average American moves every seven years. How many realtors send a Christmas card to every homeowner they've served in the past? Not many. You can do better.

Second, inform your clients about industry news and trends. Today, people are bombarded with negative news 24/7. They need to know how bad news could affect them and how to avoid negative consequences. They also want to know about positive news in your industry updates. Do this, and you'll become their "go-to" source for industry news.

Third, give your clients your best deals and guarantees. Doesn't it burn you to get screaming deals from your cable provider only to read in the fine print, "For new customer activations only." Do the opposite. Send a mailer to your customers which says, "For existing customers only." They'll feel appreciated, and you'll make sales. You should also give your clients early access to new products and services. You'll create a sense of urgency to buy now, which will make them feel special. Restaurant owners can invite regular customers to special events on the slowest night of the week. This tactic brings in more customers on a slow night and makes them feel the love.

Fourth, you lead them to act now, so they won't miss out on a great offer. People are very busy and get bombarded daily with advertising noise. If you want them to buy additional products and services from you (and you do), you must remind them again and again to take action. You can also give them more ways to make purchases, receive special limited offers, and earn better guarantees. Be a leader, and lead them to do what's in their best interest.

Finally, let's look at the opening three words, "People are silently..." Most clients will suffer in silence until they finally switch to another company. By that time, you've lost them. A few clients will take the time to complain. You must listen to your complainers. You'll learn how to improve your business and increase client retention.

Schedule time in your day to pick up the phone and call a client. Back in my corporate days, I'd hear my boss Joe call up clients and ask them, "What's exciting?" This open-ended question could go anywhere. Sometimes Joe would share a laugh or get some industry gossip. Other times he would solve an immediate business problem. Occasionally Joe would get an idea for an entirely new service. Joe's clients never felt neglected.

By staying personally connected with his Fortune 500 clients, Joe keeps his finger on the pulse of his industry and builds incredibly strong relationships with his clients. You should go and do likewise.

ACTION STEP: Think of your top five clients by revenue. Using Jay Abraham's quote as your standard, how well are you staying in touch? Call them today and ask, "What's exciting?"

Chapter 42

Know Your Clients

I am the good shepherd; and I know My sheep, and am known by My own.

—John 10:14

As a marketing consultant, I didn't want to take on a new client unless the business already had a client database. With a customer database, I could help them grow their sales by reaching out to existing clients to sell additional products and services. Without a customer database, I would have to depend far more on improving their advertising and having them spend more money on advertising.

Since you have your business as your marketing client, you must build and use your client database. The growth of your business largely depends on how well you stay connected with your past, present, and future clients. When you stay in contact, you get repeat business. When you neglect your clients, you leave clients ripe for the taking by your competitors. Don't do that!

Your client list lets you send special offers to people who bought from you in the past and are very likely to buy from you again. When you mail them more often, they'll buy from you more often. This isn't rocket science.

Who are your clients? You have past clients who no longer buy from you. You serve other clients now. You have prospects who are your future clients. You have clients who buy from you in person and (probably) other clients who buy from you online.

Let's start with the basics. You may have this information already or need help from your accountant to get it.

- Are your clients on a computer list?

- Do you have separate lists for online and in-person clients?

- How many times a year do you contact your clients?

- How much do your clients spend on an average sale?

- How many times per year does an average client buy from you?

- How many years does an average client do business with you?

The more you know about a client, the better you can stay connected with him or her. You should gather this information from your clients over time:

- Full name

- Mailing address

- Home phone

- Cell phone

- Okay to receive texts?

- Best email address

- Client status: active, inactive, prospect

- Purchase history: Dollar amount of last purchase, number of past purchases, specific products and services purchased, date of initial purchase

- Total purchases amount

- Future purchases: What specific products and services did your client express interest in?

- Birthday of client and spouse, if available

- Wedding anniversary

- Demographic information used to create avatar

- Psychographic information: Why did they buy from you?

- Interests: hobbies, children, vacations, and other personal info

- What TV shows do they like? This may seem random, but you can send Facebook Ads to prospects who like the same shows.

- Where do they get their news? Affluent baby boomers still prefer newspapers and magazines for news and information.

- Political views

You may already have a client database with this information. Good for you. Keep building your list and utilize this book to reach out to your clients. Now for the rest of you …

You may run a retail business and have no idea who your customers are. Or you just never bothered capturing names from your cash customers. Create a system to capture client names and contact information now. Enter them into your CRM software, Excel worksheet, or Google Sheets.

Here are some ways to get started:

- Ask every customer at checkout: "Can we add you to our mailing list to get special deals and announcements?"

- Hold a contest offering a valuable prize in exchange for a person's name and email address.

- Start a loyalty program like the grocery stores use.

- Go through your receipts, orders, and contracts to get names.

- Export names from your accounting program.

- Rent a mailing list; sell a low-cost item to add names for future sales.

- You should also capture the names of prospects. No business converts all their prospects into clients. Don't forget about these names, because they might try you after a bad experience with their current company.

Here are some other ways to get prospect names.

- Add prospects from every business card you collect.

- Collect prospect names and email addresses on your website.

- Get prospect contact information from your chamber's directory of members. Be careful not to abuse this list.

Don't forget to enter past clients who no longer buy from you. Later you can send them a "client reactivation letter" with a special offer to get them to come back.

Be on the lookout for opportunities to buy a competitor's business. A plumber's phone number, domain name, and customer list will have little value to a retiring plumber but a ton of value to your plumbing business. You start by sending an "announcement letter" that you have acquired certain assets of XYZ Plumbing. The retiring plumber's Yellow Pages ads will now make your phone ring. You can send a Christmas card to his former clients. You can add more names to your mailing list for practically nothing.

Jay Abraham says, "Your biggest asset is your client list." Believe it. Your clients will buy from you more often and stay with you longer if you stay in regular contact with them. Build your list and keep it fresh.

> **ACTION STEP: Think of three ways you can get more names and addresses. Choose one and use it to build your list.**

Chapter 43

Client Referral Systems

> A business without a steady flow (or even better, a
> flood!) of referrals always keeps you on the defensive,
> knowing that it's up to you to come up with new people
> to talk to.
>
> —Bob Burg, *Endless Referrals*

In this chapter, we'll look at ways to create referral systems for your business. A referral system is very different from occasionally asking a client, "Hey, do you know anyone who can benefit from my services?" Referral systems let you grow your business without spending money on advertising. You turn your best clients into your mostly unpaid sales force.

Your first step is to be referable. You need to be someone who offers a high level of service on a reliable and predictable basis. Dan Sullivan has coached entrepreneurs for over 40 years. Here are his four rules of referability.

1. Show up on time.

2. Do what you say you're going to do.

3. Finish what you start.

4. Say please and thank you.

This is not rocket science, and it's not woo-woo ninja tactics either. It's what used to be known as good manners. Make these four rules your habits, and you'll set yourself apart from your competition. Ignore these four rules, and people will stop making referrals to you. Worse yet, they'll refer people away from doing business with you.

The second step is figuring out a gift for clients who make referrals to you. Jay Abraham calls these "ethical bribes" because you're giving your clients a financial reason to make a referral. You must consider your industry, because rewarding referrals is prohibited in some industries and no big deal in many others. Real estate and mortgage have particularly tight restrictions in this area. Tanning salons have next to nothing in this area. You could give away a free week of tanning for each friend or family member referred by your tanning clients.

The third step is to give your clients referability tools. These tools can vary widely depending on your business. You don't need to choose just one. If you can offer an incentive for making a qualified referral, then include it. Here are some examples:

- Your business card with your USP and a client testimonial. Don't forget to use the back of your card.

- A flyer promoting your next seminar or other marketing event.

- A rack card is a two-sided display ad printed on glossy card stock. A rack card can be handed out or included in a business-size envelope.

- Frequent emails with interesting and valuable information. Emails can be easily forwarded.

- A free and valuable report for signing up for your email list.

Fourth, you need to determine when to ask your clients for referrals. This can be during the client service process when your client is most excited about the progress being made. This can be eliminating pain, losing weight, or making money. Or you wait until the end of the service delivery process when you've proven yourself. This can be at the close of escrow when your real estate client signs for their new home, when they've signed the tax return you completed for them, or when they pick up their dry cleaning.

You also should ask for referrals as part of your ongoing marketing to your clients. Ask your subscribers to forward your email newsletter to friends who might benefit from the service. You can ask your clients never to throw away your print newsletter—ask them to leave it in the waiting area at their doctor's office, gym, or barbershop instead.

Remember to keep it light and fun, and leave out the guilt. Let clients know how much you depend on referrals to get more great clients like them.

Fifth, once you've tested your referral process manually, you need to turn it into a system. Ideally, your staff will send out the cards and other referral reminders for you. Your staff will add new prospects to your mailing list system. Or you do this part yourself. Either way, you must remind yourself to ask for referrals, or you'll forget, and your business will suffer.

80/20 Tip: Sixth and finally, make an extra effort to turn your 20% Clients into your unofficial sales force. You want your best clients to refer their friends and family to your business to get more 20% Clients. The good news is that your dissatisfied clients will not refer their friends, so you won't get more of those types of clients.

Attorney Referral System

Here is a referral system for an attorney. You can adapt this simple system to your business by printing this on the back of your business card:

> Unlike most other attorneys, I don't buy expensive advertising to get new clients. Instead, I get my new clients from satisfied clients like you.
>
> Please give my card to a friend who might need my services. They'll get a free initial consultation, and you'll be entered into my annual drawing for an iPad Pro.
>
> Thank you very much.
>
> Referred by _____

When a prospect comes in with your business card with a name on it, trade it for a card with a blank referral space. If they come in without a card, ask them, "Who referred you to me?" Write the name on one of your cards.

Next, put the card with their friend's name into a fishbowl. There will be lots of other cards. This sends the message that you get lots of referrals from your many satisfied clients. Mention in a very casual way, "If you're happy with my services I hope you refer me to your friends. You might win the iPad Pro this year. Now let's talk about your situation ..."

An iPad Pro or Apple Watch is a small cost compared to the number of referrals you receive. You can send a letter with a "second place" prize for everyone who didn't get the main prize. This prize can be a "Buy 1 entrée, get the 2nd free" at a popular restaurant in your city. You become a referral partner with that restaurant and help them get new patrons. A win-win deal for everybody.

Home Builder Referral System

I recently attended a business conference and met Karen who sells homes for Simplicity Homes. Her company takes all the uncertainty and anxiety out of building a home on your bare dirt lot. They have an amazing website to help people decide what house to buy and how much it will cost. You can visit their website at simplicity-homes.com.

At the event, Karen told me about their referral program. After introductions, Karen didn't ask me if I planned to build a new home. Instead, she told me her company would pay me $500 if I sent someone to them who builds a Simplicity Home. That got my attention. She handed me her business card backside-up. I noticed this friendly reminder on the back of her card:

Thanks you can take to the Bank!

For every person you send our way who builds
a Simplicity Home, you will receive $500.
See program guidelines online.

The next day, I sent an email to my friend Evan, who had just sold his home for $10,000 above appraisal. He sold it FSBOWHFR which stands for "For Sale By Owner With Help From Richard." He was a hot prospect for Simplicity Homes, so I told him all about them and sent him Karen's contact information.

Now let me ask you something:

Are you thinking about building a new home in Washington, Oregon, or Northern California? If you answered "Yes!" take a look at Simplicity-Homes.com. Ask for Karen when you call for more information. Be sure to tell her "Richard Emmons sent me."

Do you see the power of referral systems? If Karen didn't have a referral system in place, she might not have handed me her card. I probably would have forgotten to tell Evan about her company. I wouldn't have used them as an example in my book. I became a part of Simplicity's marketing and sales team because of a simple win-win client referral system.

With client referral systems in place, you can reduce your advertising expenses substantially—perhaps even to zero. Some businesses only accept new clients by referral.

To learn more about setting up referral systems for your business, I recommend you study chapter 11 of Jay Abraham's book, *Getting Everything You Can Out of All You've Got.*

☐ **ACTION STEP: Do you have one or more referral systems now? If not, it's time to order more business cards.**

Chapter 44

Lifetime Value of Clients

He who can spend the most to acquire a customer, wins.
—Dan Kennedy

When you know how much a client is worth to you over time, you know how much you can spend to acquire a new client. Some companies even spend 100% of the initial sale. Why would you do this? You make an initial sale to add that buyer to your marketing database and sell to them again and again in the future.

In *Getting Everything You Can Out of All You've Got*, Jay Abraham defined lifetime value of clients as the "total profit of an average client over the lifetime of his or her patronage–including all residual sales–less all advertising, marketing, and incremental product or service fulfillment expenses."

There are numerous ways to calculate your lifetime customer value ("LCV"). We will use a simple formula in this chapter. You do not need an exact calculation to begin using LCV in your business.

How much is an average client worth to you each year? You calculate this by dividing your annual profit by the number of active clients. For example, $200,000 annual profit divided by 100 active clients means each client contributes $2000 profit per year. This is the "annual profit" or "AP" amount.

On average, how many years does a typical client buy from you? You or your bookkeeper will need to dig through your accounting program to figure this out. If you run a retail store with a lot of cash customers, you can survey your customers at check out: "How long have you been doing business with us?" Either way, this is worth the effort and only needs to be done once. This is called "client duration" or CD.

Let's assume that your clients do business with you for five years on average. You calculate your lifetime client value by multiplying annual profit by client duration.

$$LCV = AP \times CD$$

In this example LCV equals $2,000 x 5 or $10,000. You now know that every new client is worth $10,000 to your business.

Let's see how knowing the lifetime value of clients affects the marketing in a few different industries. You can apply this to your business and learn how much you can spend to get a new client.

Financial Advisor

Let's assume you typically earn 1% on a client with one million dollars invested with you. Your typical client stays with you for ten years. This is $10,000 per year or $100,000 LCV. You could spend $10,000 to get this client and earn $90,000 net over the next ten years. You spend $10,000 to get $100,000 in revenue. You would have a 10:1 MROI or "marketing return on investment." $10,000 would pay for a nice client appreciation dinner. Be sure to read Chapter 54 to learn how to use client dinners to get new clients.

Pizza Restaurant

A family can easily spend $50 on pizza, salad, and drinks. They might go out for pizza 20 times per year. This adds up to $1,000 over the year. Over a five-year period, they could spend $5000 at your restaurant. That represents a lot of pizza and a lot of profit.

Knowing LCV lets the pizza restaurant owner calculate how much to spend to get them to come the very first time. You can offer a special deal for families which bring in another family. You want families to build a habit of coming to your restaurant for special events such as birthday parties. You also can justify sponsoring a local softball team because they will visit your restaurant after every game. Especially if you pay for special jerseys.

Web Hosting

Some businesses are stickier than others because they are easy to start doing business with but a pain in the neck to leave. These companies can spend even more to get a new client because they know that the client won't leave for a long time.

Web hosting companies take advantage of this stickiness factor. Imagine a website developer who creates a dozen WordPress websites per year for five years. Everything is running smoothly for his clients. He might pay $500 per year on web hosting services. Would he move to another web hosting company to save $50 per year? Not likely, because he would have to migrate 60 websites to the new host. It's a lot of work, and things can go sideways. It's just not worth making a move to save $50 a year.

Web hosting companies know this, and you see it in their marketing. They happily pay affiliate commissions, i.e., finders fees, for up to 100% or more of the initial annual service fees. Web hosting companies also give a sizeable discount to the customer for the first year of hosting. They understand lifetime client value and acquire new clients using this market intelligence.

80/20 Tip: You can explode the profitability of your business when you calculate the lifetime value of your 20% Clients who generate 80% of your sales and profits. You may discover that your top 20% Clients generate profit of $5,000 per year and stay with you for ten years. Your remaining 80% of clients generate $2,000 profit per year on average and stay with you for only five years.

Let's calculate the difference in lifetime client value for this example:

Client Group	Annual Profit	Duration	LCV
Top 20%	$5,000	10	$50,000
Other 80%	$2,000	5	$10,000

Knowing the lifetime value of your 20% Clients makes it clear where you should focus your marketing efforts and dollars. You should make more personal contact with your 20% Clients. You should invite them to special "by invitation only" events. Yes, all clients are special, but some clients are more special than others.

You should still market to the other 80% clients on your list. You never want to neglect any of your clients. Some of your 20% Clients will move away, pass away, or simply get away from you through no fault of your own. You should nurture those in the 80% group because some of them will move into the 20% group in the future. You have no guaranteed way to know who will move up, so you should still market your entire mailing list.

Jay Abraham said that "whenever I got a new client, the first question I asked was 'what's the lifetime value of clients?'" Now is the time to know that answer for your own business.

> **ACTION STEP: Calculate the lifetime value of your clients. If you can calculate this for your 20% Clients, give yourself a gold star.**

Chapter 45

Reconnect With Past Clients

> The easiest possible way to increase your client base is laughably obvious, but hardly anyone does it. You can instantly increase your number of clients by regaining your inactive clients.
>
> —Jay Abraham

People start doing business with you and your business because they know, like, and trust you and what you offer. At some point, some of these people stop doing business with you. Before we look at how to get back past clients, let's look at how improving client retention, i.e., reducing client attrition, can boost your business growth rate.

Your client attrition rate is the percentage of clients who stop doing business with you each year. Sometimes because of neglect. Sometimes slow service. Many times, they just got out of the habit of doing business with you. Or they dealt with a rude employee you fired six months ago. Many of these past clients can be reactivated.

Your client attrition rate directly impacts your growth rate. If you lose 20% of your clients each year, you need to add 30% new clients to generate an overall increase of 10% client base growth. What happens to your growth rate if you reduce your attrition rate by 10%?

	Current	Improved
Clients at start of year	100	100
Client base growth	+30% or +30	+30% or +30
Client attrition	-20% or -20	-10% or -10
Clients at end of year	110	120
Client base net growth	10%	20%

By cutting the attrition rate, you double your growth rate from 10% to 20%. Going forward you need to improve your client services to stop losing as many clients. That's why we spend so much time in this book on staying connected with your client.

Now imagine a company wanting to grow its client base by 20% over the next year. The company typically loses 25% of its clients each year. This company would need to add 45% new clients to offset the lost clients. By reducing the client attrition rate to 10%, the company can reach its client growth target with only 30% new clients. The company can spend less on advertising.

	Current	Improved
Clients at start of year	100	100
Client base growth	+45% or +45	+30% or +30
Client attrition	-25% or -25	-10% or -10
Clients at end of year	120	120
Client base net growth	20%	20%

Now let's look at how to turn inactive clients into active clients.

How to Reactivate Past Clients

You can reactivate past clients with a personal visit, by calling them, or by sending them a personal letter or postcard. If all you have are email addresses, then send a series of emails to get them to buy again. You must make it personal, caring, and authentic, however you contact them.

Your first step is to compile a list of inactive clients. You want to know who they are, when they stopped doing business with you, and why they stopped doing business with you.

Do you really need to know why a client stopped doing business with you? Yes, if your clients spend thousands of dollars with you each year. A personal visit or phone call would be best—from you, a manager, or one of your salespeople. If you have thousands of low-value past clients, i.e. $100 per year, then keep it simple and get basic contact information into your database. You can get started with an email address only.

Your second step is to devise a special offer to get them back. This will vary depending on your business and why they stopped doing business with you. If you discover a problem, then fix it immediately and at your cost. For other reasons, your special offer can be an upgrade, a new product, a free meal, or a free service, i.e., teeth cleaning. Whether you are a dentist, pool cleaner, restaurant, or retailer, you offer them an ethical bribe to get them back.

80/20 Tip: You should make personal calls to past clients who used to be in your top 20%. On the phone, you can listen to them and understand what went wrong before. If your business was at fault, you can say, "I'd really like a second chance to make this right. Can I offer you a special deal as our way of saying 'We're sorry'?" Many times, a personal invitation to come back is all it takes. You may find out that they left for greener pastures and it turned out to have dead grass colored with green spray paint. They were too embarrassed to call you up, so your call gets the relationship back on track.

What if the person no longer needs your service? That's okay. Ask them if they know anyone who might need your service. Getting referrals from past 20% Clients is another way to grow your business.

You can also have a staff member make the calls on your behalf.

- For chiropractors, the receptionist can call patients who haven't had an appointment for eight months. "You haven't been in for a while, and the doctor is concerned about your back ..."

- For pool cleaners, an assistant can make calls to past owners who stopped using your pool cleaning service in the past. "The summer is heating up, and Bob is concerned about your water quality ..."

- For boutique clothing retailers, a sales clerk can call past clients in between walk-in customers. "Hi, Jill. You haven't been here in a while. I want to let you know about an upcoming sale for customers only. Would you like me to send you a flyer?"

For many businesses, you can keep it simple and mail your entire list of past clients. You should assume they are among the 68% who felt neglected by you and went elsewhere.

Reactivation Letter Template

Here's an ad structure for your client reactivation letter.

Headline: "What did we do wrong?" Or "We Miss You!"

Lead paragraph: "We haven't heard from you in a while." Weave in your USP to highlight why you are better than your competitors. Let them know how you're benefiting your clients now. Including one or two client testimonials will add proof to your story. Tell them you want them back as a client, and ask them to give you a chance to make it right.

Offer: Make a great offer as described above.

Call to action: Give them a call to action to come by your office and bring this letter, go to a special landing page, or call and mention it to the receptionist.

The advantage of sending a postcard or email is that you'll only hear from the people who say, "Yes!" You can repeat this same mailing every six months and slowly reactivate past clients. However, when you successfully reactivate a past client, you must absolutely, positively remove them from your inactive client list. Otherwise, you'll send them another reactivation postcard, and they won't feel the love.

Make it as easy as possible for these past clients to start doing business with you again. Be sure to tell your employees about this marketing campaign so they will turn on the charm and over-deliver on the service.

The longer you've been in business, the more past clients you can reactivate. Don't be embarrassed about how you may have neglected these clients in the past. View this as a golden opportunity to help them now. You'll grow your business without spending much money on advertising. You'll find this far less expensive than attracting cold prospects who need to be converted into clients.

> **ACTION STEP: Identify your inactive clients from your client database. Create a generous offer to win them back. Send it to 100 inactive clients and test the results. If the promotion pays for itself, then send another 100.**

Chapter 46

Your Website, Your Platform

> The web is more a social creation than a technical one. I
> designed it for a social effect—to help people work
> together—and not as a technical toy.
> —Sir Tim Berners-Lee, inventor of the World Wide Web

Got a business card? Got a telephone? Got a website? There will come a time in the 21st century when a company without a website will seem impossible. Or ridiculous. Like being a service professional today without a business card. Or a phone.

Is this you? You're not alone. I used to get solid referrals from financial wholesalers, and often all I had was a name and a phone number. Before I called an advisor, I tried to find him on the internet. Sometimes I couldn't find him at all. Many, many times I find him in all sorts of directory sites which pull from white pages listings and public directory sites. They may be on their broker-dealer website along with the firm's other 10,000 financial advisors. The harder it is to find them, the more I know they need my help.

Imagine one of your clients referring you to a good friend or relative. What if they don't feel like picking up the telephone and giving you a call? They'll check you out on the internet first. What will they find? If they don't find you on the web, they may not bother calling you at all. Your website offers a great way for prospects to get to know you before they meet with you.

If your business doesn't have a website, I strongly encourage that you get one up and running, and do it now. Much more on how to do this later in this chapter.

Now you may be telling yourself, "I've had a website since 2001!" Good enough? No. Many businesses have websites which look dated, haven't changed since they went up, and are invisible to search engines. Is that you?

You Own Your Website

You might say to yourself, "Well, duh—and it's a pain the neck." Yes, you need to maintain and update your business website. This takes time and money. Your Facebook business page, Google My Business page, Bing page, and Yelp page seem to take care of themselves and are free.

Yet there is a big difference with your company website: You own it. You're in control. Your website can reflect your personality and your company's culture. With some effort, you can keep your website fresh, informative, and legally compliant for your industry. You'll give prospects a good first impression, and clients will come back later for more information.

You may have a fantastic Facebook page, Google My Business page, and YouTube channel. Good for you. However, you need to see these platforms as "rented" websites. Your digital landlord can change your "lease terms" at any time. "Free rent" can become very costly. Forget about 30-day notice; you might get "Google slapped" and get no notice. Let's review how the terms of your "lease" changed at Facebook over the years.

In the beginning, Facebook let you set up a free business page. You posted updates about what's going on in your business and about your products and services. Everyone who "liked" your page saw your updates. Next, Facebook began reducing how many followers saw your updates. Facebook began offering you the ability to pay to "boost" your post. Now, maybe 2 or 3% of your followers will see your post unless you boost (aka, advertise) it. This could be just one out of every 50 followers. Boosting your page updates costs money, which means you're paying to advertise to your existing clients.

Contrast this with having those same 50 followers as subscribers on your email list. 100% will see your emails land in their inbox. Most will open your email when your emails are consistently interesting and add a little value for the reader. You can offer a deal or an opportunity with every email. Links take them back to your website. Again, you're in control with your website and your email list.

Mobile Rules

These days you must be your own marketing consultant to avoid website design malpractice. This occurs when a business owner hires a web designer to build a new or improved website. All seems well until someone looks at the website on a smartphone. Then it looks something like this:

Mobile Rules

These days you must be your own marketing consultant to avoid website malpractice. This occurs when a business owner hires a web designer to build a new or improved website. All looks good until someone looks at the website on a smartphone. Then it looks something like this:

Many websites use the same layout, information, and menus regardless of the device—even when shrunken down to fit a 4, 5, or 6 inch screen. A content rich yet unreadable website on a smartphone means far fewer prospects.

On April 21, 2015, Google announced that mobile-friendly websites would get a boost in mobile search results. This change was referred to as "Mobilegeddon" because millions of mobile-unfriendly websites fell in search rankings overnight. They had to be redesigned or suffer lower search results.

This happened because website design had always centered on the computer user's experience, not tablet or smartphone users. Now web designers take a "mobile first" design strategy to ensure the website works well for mobile users as well as tablets and large computer monitors. A responsive web design ensures a website looks and functions well on every type of device.

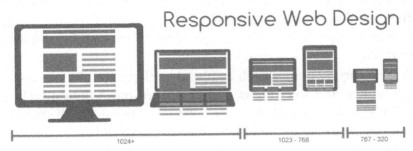

Responsive Web Design

Google did businesses a favor back then, because many people now use their smartphone as their sole computing device.

You can test your website here: https://search.google.com/test/mobile-friendly.

Did your website pass? Kudos to your web designer. Not so good?

No worries. With your USP, client testimonials, and avatar-focused marketing, you have many good reasons to refresh your website now.

Now let's look at different types of websites.

Types of Websites

Authority Websites are also known as brochure websites because they replaced printed color brochures. Today, static content won't get people to come back and find out what's new. When prospects "check you out" online, your authority website is where you want them to learn more about you.

Professional service providers such as lawyers, insurance agents, engineers, CPAs, and advisors generally don't sell anything from their websites. The marketing goal is to get a qualified prospect in the office for an initial consultation. For lawyers, your website's primary purpose is to inform prospects about your firm and their options. You also want clients to come back for additional information about other services you offer. You answer the question, "Why do you need a lawyer?" by explaining how you can help them win in court or successfully deal with an insurance company. You describe your staff and their qualifications. You may have a blog with news and case studies. You offer several ways for potential clients to get in touch with your office.

"Blue Collar" service providers such as plumbers and carpet cleaners offer immediate solutions for major problems, i.e., stopped-up pipes and flood damage. You must make it easy for someone to get in touch now, especially when your prospect is on the road and using a smartphone.

Creative professionals such as photographers, graphic designers, videographers, and wedding consultants need more than merely an authority website. You must have a website design which makes it easy for prospects to see your portfolio and be wowed.

Retail shops should help the prospect feel the experience of shopping in your store and why they should come in and take a look.

One-Page Websites work well for new service professionals without many testimonials, clients, services, or a story. The homepage is the only page. You include a dramatic image, a compelling headline about how the professional can help (think USP), services offered, contact information, and testimonials on one long webpage.

This website type is perfect for mobile users because visitors don't have the time or interest to read lots of information. Be sure to include easy ways for site visitors to click to call, text, or send an email to you.

Landing Pages, aka Sales Pages. When someone clicks on an offer link in an email, Facebook ad, Google AdWords ad, or banner ad, the person needs to "land" somewhere. This landing zone should not be your main website, because the person will wander all over your main website. A landing page gives the viewer one choice to make. This choice can be to click, call, sign up for an email newsletter, or read another call to action.

A landing page must give the prospect more information about the offer seen in the advertisement. Here's an example of how this works:

Financial planner John Smith announces a living trust seminar using Facebook ads targeting local retirees.

The Facebook ad shows a picture of a worried retired couple. The headline is "Worried about the embarrassment of probate?" The CTA could be "Free seminar provides answers. Click for details ..."

An interested person clicks the ad, which takes them to a single purpose landing page such as JohnSmithCFP.com/seminar or AbolishProbateIowa.com. The landing page is a sales letter focused on getting the prospect to call the office to RSVP for the seminar. That's it. The landing page can include far more detail than would fit on a small digital ad. And focus only on the seminar.

Landing pages can be all text or include a sales video to explain the offer. The "Buy" button should stand out (orange normally works best) and be labeled to match the offer, such as "Subscribe Now," "Buy Now!", "Reserve Your Seat," "Get Access Now," and so on.

Lead Pages are one-page websites used to collect prospect name and email addresses. This is a "two-step" sales process. Step one is getting the email address. Step two is sending additional information about the product or service along with a link to buy the product or service. You must give the person a reason to opt in, because most people are overloaded with emails already. You do this by giving away something with high perceived value, usually a PDF report, eBook, or video mini-course.

Lead page services such as leadpages.net and instapage.com make it easy to create these types of landing pages. Domain Names are cheap, so your lead page can have a different and easier-to-remember website address.

Ecommerce Websites let your prospects make their first purchase and your clients buy again and again. The distinction between brick-and-mortar "commerce" and online "ecommerce" is disappearing because so many companies do both now.

People can go to Walmart.com to research products, read reviews, and buy online. Then they drive to the store to pick up the product. Is this commerce or ecommerce?

Buying products and services on your website must be easy for your clients or they'll head over to Amazon, Walmart, Costco, eBay, or elsewhere.

Publisher Websites like Wikipedia publish information in a way which is very easy for the reader to consume. Little or nothing is sold on these types of website.

Zillow provides an enormous amount of information about houses yet does not (yet) let you click and buy a home or do auctions like eBay. Zillow sells leads to real estate agents and mortgage brokers.

Membership Websites require visitors to log in to see information, how-to videos, and other non-public information. Often you can add a membership section to your existing website for your clients.

Now let's look at what your authority website should contain.

Professional Websites

You may already have a fantastic website which is loved by your clients and frequently visited by prospects who soon become your clients. I assume you made it even better by adding your newly created USP. Congratulations!

For the rest of you, let's go over the basics of professional websites. You can adapt these ideas to your business to improve the results of your website.

Responsive Design means your website layout adjusts to the size screen of your viewer. This includes smartphones, tablets, laptops, desktops with huge monitors, and Super Bowl-sized wall-mounted big screen TVs. Remember that many people will never see your website on a computer or even a tablet. This is helpful for most businesses, because a minimalist website costs less than a full-blown website project of the past with so much screen space to fill.

Your Home Page is a Sales Page. By default, many websites have a list of blog posts as the home page. You can improve the usefulness of your website homepage by formatting it as a sales page. This structure includes a powerful headline, body copy, and a call to action, i.e., call your office.

Segment your prospects on the home page. This new approach seeks to move visitors onto different paths depending on their main need. A real estate broker could ask visitors, "How can we help you?" Three large buttons offer three distinct groups of prospects:

- I'm a first-time homebuyer

- My growing family needs more space

- I want to downsize for retirement

How can this help you? Each button links to a specific page on your website. You provide helpful information for this type of prospect. You offer a free report to these visitors in exchange for their email address.

For instance, the first-time homebuyer gets a report about the pitfalls and opportunities of homeownership. This first-time homebuyer would receive a series of email messages (aka, an "autoresponder") which could go out every day for ten days. You also add them to your regular email list. Every email would encourage them to call you for more information and get questions answered. A separate report and autoresponder series would be sent out for growing families and downsizing couples.

Easy Navigation. On mobile devices, the navigation menu typically appears after clicking on an icon of three horizontal bars. This design prevents menu items from covering up the main headline or action step on the home page. On computers, you have more room for a navigation bar, but don't overdo it.

In the old days, companies would have two navigation bars at the top of the screen. Now, smarter companies minimize the navigation choices at the top of the screen and load up the footer with detailed and helpful links about the company. Taken to an extreme, the "upside down landing page" puts all the menu items in the footer, so the visitor sees your headline at the top and then sales copy.

Whatever you do, make it easy for your website visitors. Advanced design tip: Easy comes from making things simple, not complicated.

Opt-in Box To Collect Email Addresses. You need to collect email addresses, so you can follow up with additional information and offers to turn prospects into clients.

Give visitors a valuable report, coupon, free sample, or another freebie to "ethically bribe" them into giving you their email address. If you can make a low-cost initial sale, these email addresses will be more valuable because the person gave you money in addition to their email address.

If you sell to people based in Europe, you must comply with new privacy regulations known as GDPR or General Data Protection Regulation. These requirements went into effect on May 25, 2018.

Keep It Interesting. You can be entertaining. You can be informative. You can be both and be "infotaining." However, you should never be boring, or your website visitors will click away.

Be Easy on the Eyes. One of the benefits of mobile-friendly design has been the elimination of complicated website layouts with too many competing images and headlines. If your site is cluttered, first-time site visitors may get confused, click away and never come back.

Some websites keep an older look intentionally as part of their brand. One top news site has not changed its layout since 1998: DrudgeReport.com. It's not ugly; it's a classic. Don't confuse this with having a 2011 look which screams, "Don't even think about looking at me on your iPhone. Please." Thankfully, modern website theme designs make having a good design easier than ever before.

Your Website is an Advertisement. Be sure to remember that your website visitors are tuned into WII-FM, so keep everything relevant to your prospects and clients. It's not about you.

Your site will be more SEO-friendly when you have lots of helpful information. SEO stands for "search engine optimization." When people enter words related to your business into Google, Bing, DuckDuckGo, or other search engines, you want your business to appear on the top of the search results. When they click on your link, you get "organic traffic" to your website. Organic traffic is free traffic, whereas Google Ads traffic is "paid traffic."

Information Pages. Nearly every website will have these pages accessible from the header and possibly the footer navigation bars.

Services. This page lists all of your services. Each service can have a separate page. Add some testimonials for each service. Make these pages helpful and interesting, and Google will help get people to your website. And your clients will be more likely to share your pages with their friends and social media sites.

Resources. Your resources page can have helpful and free tools for your prospects and clients. Financial advisors can include articles, a glossary of financial terms, videos, retirement calculators, and more.

Blog. This link will take readers to your page of articles. You keep your website helpful, relevant, and fresh by writing blog posts about industry news, client success stories, and more. You'll find more article ideas in Chapter 52 when we cover print newsletters. When you write a long post, break up the text with subheads, pictures, infographics, and charts to keep the reader engaged.

About. The About page may be about you only, you and your staff, your business, or a combination. Don't use this page to tell your life story. The "About" story relates to how you can solve the problems of your clients, along with company history and information. See Chapter 16 for how to write a biography which sells.

Staff. You may want a separate page for your staff biographies. Be sure to keep the staff page current. Also, ask your staff members to sign a release if you use their picture on your website or brochures. One of my receptionists left my company and insisted I no longer show her on the website. Photoshop came to the rescue to make her disappear. I'm glad it wasn't a video.

Contact. You want to make it easy for people to contact you. At a minimum, provide a contact box so people can email questions and comments to you. You can have your business address, phone number, fax number (depending on your avatar), chat window, Skype number, and other ways you can be reached.

You should not show an email address, because spambots will add you to their list. Spammers tune into WII-FM and only care about themselves, so don't make it easy for them.

Legal Pages vary widely depending on your industry. Look at major players in your industry for ideas on what's needed. Every website should have Privacy Policy and Terms and Conditions pages.

Privacy Policy. Your privacy policy explains what information you collect from users of your website and what you do with it. Most websites use very generic privacy policy language. However, things are getting much more specific since the GDPR went into effect on May 25, 2018.

Google's privacy policy is summarized here and explained in many pages of details elsewhere. Notice that the effective date is the same date that GDPR went into effect. Not a coincidence.

> When you use our services, you're trusting us with your information. We understand this is a big responsibility and work hard to protect your information and put you in control.
>
> This Privacy Policy is meant to help you understand what information we collect, why we collect it, and how you can update, manage, export, and delete your information.
>
> Effective May 25, 2018   Archived versions   Download PDF

Terms and Conditions. This page is also named "Terms of Use" or "Terms of Service." According to DisclaimerTemplate.com, a website's terms and conditions "governs a user's legal rights about the website and provides the website owner with control over their legal relationship with their visitors, members, and clients. If your website or blog provides services, products, content, advice or opinions, you should have a terms and conditions [page] to protect you and your business by limiting your legal liability."

Earnings Disclosure. If you make any claims about making money on your website, then you need to have an Earnings Disclosure page.

Other Legal Pages. Other legal pages are required for industries such as medical and real estate. You should study your biggest competitors to find out what they think is required for your business—and then check the law.

Paid Legal Page Documents. In the past, I relied upon WordPress plugins for my legal pages. With GDPR requirements and Facebook data breaches in 2018, this isn't good enough anymore. You can use an experienced attorney for these documents or get them online.

Here is one source for attorney-drafted website documents: https://www.disclaimertemplate.com/. Yes, I read their Terms of Use page, and learned I could use their templates on up to three websites. This company has a package deal for the Privacy Policy, Terms of Use, and Earnings Disclosure pages now priced for $118 or $147 with an annual update. https://www.disclaimertemplate.com/the-big-3/. For under $700, this same company will customize these documents for you.

Keep Your Website Current: Part 1

Go to your website now. Check the footer. Does it say "© 2018 ABC Company"? That was last year. An old copyright year makes a website appear dated instantly. Many companies miss this every year. Take a look and fix this now, if necessary. Then mark your calendar for the next update on December 31. Better yet, add some code or a plugin to keep it current automatically.

I use my footer to let people know how long I've been in business:

© 2006-2019 by Richard Emmons and Reality Marketing LLC

I checked Amazon.com's footer, and they do the same thing:

© 1996-2019, Amazon.com, Inc. or its affiliates

Keep Your Website Current: Part 2

Now let's look at how to keep the other 99% of your website current.

Blog Articles. If your blog posts are dated, make sure you have current articles. You can hide dates if you're not adding new articles now. Better to add some new articles. With a WordPress website, you can change the publication date to make your older, yet timeless, articles appear at the top of the list.

About. Review your About page at least once per year and keep it current. You want people to know, like, and trust you from this page.

You also want them to buy something from you, so keep it relevant to your target audience. Also, make sure your headshot is new enough that prospects will recognize you when they meet you in person.

Events. Use your website to promote *future* events. Do not use your website to memorialize *past* events. For completed events, add copy above the headline to encourage your readers to join your mailing list to be notified of future events.

Products and Services. Whenever you update your products and services, you need to make sure that your agreements, ads, flyers, and website reflect the changes.

Videos. Many websites use "video sales letters" to sell products and services. You can also use videos to personalize your site; for instance, explain why you started your company and how you help your clients. In this case, the KISS principle stands for keeping it simple (and) short. Simple means don't overcomplicate your message. Short means under three minutes long.

Are you a service professional, such as an auto mechanic or plumber? Consider a section with DIY videos showing how to do basic repairs. You position yourself as an expert by demonstrating you know what you are doing. Many people will think it's too complicated and give you a call so you can do it for them.

Keep It Secure with SSL. Huh? SSL means every page on your website begins with HTTPS and not HTTP. HTTP stands for "hypertext transport protocol." The "S" stands for security. According to Google, "HTTPS protects the integrity of your website" and "protects the privacy and security of your users" and "is the future of the web."

Before 2018, you needed HTTPS only when you sold something on your website. HTTPS was a geeky extra for brochure sites. In July 2018, Google began penalizing websites using HTTP by calling them "Non-secure" on the address bar of your browser. If your website visitors see "non-secure," they'll leave your site and go elsewhere. When your website has HTTPS, Chrome and other browsers will show your website as secure.

To make your website secure, you need to install an SSL certificate. This used to cost money. Now free SSL certificates will protect most business websites. You should call your website host and ask them for help with this.

One more thing. Being your own marketing consultant does not mean getting geeky and building and fixing your website by yourself. When you have a problem, ask for help. Let techies do what they do best. You want to focus on marketing your business and taking care of your clients.

> **ACTION STEP:** Test your website on mobile devices. Did your website pass the test?

Chapter 47

Does Your Website Need a Makeover?

Design is not just what it looks like and feels like. Design is
how it works.

—Steve Jobs

Let's consider the current state of your website. There are three
possibilities:

1. "I have a new, responsive, mobile-optimized website, and it
   only needs some copywriting tweaks."

2. "I don't have a website."

3. "I have an outdated website which looks terrible on
   smartphones and tablets."

Scenario #1: "My website needs some copywriting tweaks."

This scenario is the easiest to fix. You improve your website the same
way you improve all your current advertising:

1. Incorporate your unique selling proposition. With mobile-
   friendly design, you put your most powerful message at the
   top. Your USP tells prospects why they should do business
   with you rather than your competitor. Your USP also reminds
   clients why they should stay with you and not look elsewhere.

2. Improve headlines on all pages.

3. Add subheads to guide the reader. Many people skim and scan
   today.

4. Make your offer clear and emotionally compelling.

5. Add testimonials to your site—the ones you collect during the
   USP creation process. Especially focus on testimonials from

20% Clients.

6. Make your call to action clear, emotionally compelling, and easy to do.

Scenario #2: "I don't have a website."

If you don't have a website, your job is obvious. You need to get one and quickly. Yet not in haste—you wouldn't build a house without a plan. This is also true with a website.

Plan Your Website

You need to know what you want in your website and have a plan to achieve it. Start with this list and carefully review what we covered in chapter 46.

1. What is your website objective? This means knowing what you want the website to achieve. Will it be primarily for your clients? Or for your prospects? Brochure site only? Or ecommerce?

2. What will be your website structure? This includes the menus, pages, and content of your website. Will you sell products or services? Do you need a shopping cart? Will you want a members-only area? A discussion forum?

3. What will be your call to action? Your CTA can be opting into an email list, calling in for an appointment, or clicking to buy now.

4. Write the copy for all your pages. This includes the home page, about page, services pages, and other pages. You need this whether you create the website or hire someone to build it.

5. Gather any images to help tell your story and bring life to your website. We hired a professional photographer to take photographs of the building and inside The Boardroom. We saw the $1,800 fee as an investment which would support our marketing efforts for years.

6. This includes pictures of you and your staff members. Ideally, you have a brick wall or other backdrop which you'll use for all pictures now and in the future when you hire new employees.

Be sure to give your staff members several days' notice of the photo session. Don't say I didn't warn you if your photographer shows up unannounced to take staff photos, and your staff revolts.

Who Should Build Your Website?

You now have a plan and the elements needed to create your website. Now you need to decide to build and maintain it yourself or hire someone to do one or both for you. Don't miss the "and maintain it" part. Websites are like billboards: You pay upfront to design it and pay monthly to continue to have it. Your website may be your primary advertising platform on the internet. Why would you expect to pay nothing to keep it live and maintain it? Better than a billboard, you can change your website to keep it current.

Thankfully, the term "webmaster" died along with dial-up internet. In the old days, any changes to your website had to be done by the webmaster. It was a big deal, cost money, and often didn't happen because no one wanted to deal with the webmaster. In a real sense, we were the web slaves. Glad those days are over with new content management systems like WordPress.

Can you create your own website? Maybe. A better question is "Should you build your own website?"

For most sole practitioners, I would answer yes on one condition: You don't use WordPress. Instead, you use a website builder. Why not use WordPress when over 30% of the world's top 10 million websites run on it? Do you really have time for a hobby now? You don't have time to learn everything you need to know about WordPress to have an effective, up-to-date, and safe website. (Safe? You need to back up your website and keep it protected from hackers. We cover this at the end of this chapter.)

WordPress Or a Website Builder?

A website builder is the better option for many small businesses these days. I'll explain why in a minute.

I've used WordPress for over ten years, and I love its flexibility and power. WordPress has come a long way since its release in 2003 by Matt Mullenweg and Mike Little. WordPress began as a blogging platform, and now businesses use it for nearly every kind of website imaginable. You can change the design by changing the theme. You can improve the functionality by adding free and paid plugins. You can increase website security with anti-hacking and backup plugins. You can effectively make a WordPress website do just about anything these days.

However, WordPress is not for everyone. Adding all that power and flexibility has made it much more complicated to set up and maintain. It can be overkill.

I came to this conclusion while creating the "Launch Your Business" course for the Ron Paul Curriculum. One of my course objectives was teaching the students how to create WordPress websites. This process includes choosing a web hosting company, getting a domain name, installing WordPress, installing a theme, adding plugins, setting up email accounts using cPanel (whatever that is), creating pages, menus, and a whole lot more.

I used ten lessons (out of 180) to teach this. Later in the course, I spend another five lessons teaching students how to use website builders to create websites. Website builders such as Squarespace, Weebly and Duda let non-techies create websites in a hosted setting without the complexity of WordPress.org. You can also use WordPress in a hosted setting at WordPress.com. Stay with me in case your eyes are beginning to glaze over.

I teach my students about many different types of businesses, such as photography, copywriting, and app creation. These students do not need a WordPress.org website to promote their service businesses. A website builder would save them time and money and eliminate the technical aspects of having a website. This may be true for you as well.

Some of my students plan to build websites for local businesses. These students need to have a deep understanding of WordPress.org, because WordPress.org offers the most flexibility and power in a website platform.

If you decide to use WordPress, you should pay for a premium theme such as Thrive Themes. Free themes are often limited in functionality, lack timely updates or support when you need help. Many themes are abandoned. Premium themes get added features and stay current with new releases of WordPress. You need great technical support because you don't have the time to waste figuring it out yourself. You get what you pay for, so pay for it.

Again, you must plan your website before choosing your website platform, i.e., WordPress or a website builder. You must write the copy and gather the images before you can hire a website developer or begin to do it yourself. You must know what you want your prospects and clients to do and see at your website. Otherwise, you may go down a wrong path and waste your time and money.

More Reasons To Hire a Website Developer

A detailed plan for your website also helps you hire a qualified website developer to build your website for you. This person can also maintain the website for you. For not a lot of money, in most cases, you can get a great website without having to tackle the technical learning curves of doing it yourself. Make sure you tell the web designer that you want to be able to add posts, i.e., articles, and make tweaks to the website copy.

Outsourcing this task to a freelancer or small business in your community can take a long-term headache off your plate. You want to focus on growing your business and providing superb service to your clients. You don't want to get tangled up in technical knots because you're the resident website guru.

Do you do the payroll tax accounting for your company? Most owners realize it's too important, too technical, and too time-consuming, to handle on their own: They hire a payroll specialist. What does that have to do with websites? Seems obvious, but I've seen many a one-person startup spends months building a WordPress website. The final result is painful to look at and could have been achieved quickly and cheaply with a website builder. Or outsourced to a local website developer. This time would have been better invested on creating a USP which would help all forms of advertising.

You want to be able to go on vacations and not be interrupted— whether the interruption is because paydays happen, or websites need system updates.

Scenario #3: "My website looks terrible on mobile."

Most of what I wrote for Scenario #2 is also true when you have a website which needs a lot of work. Or you may have a newer website which tanks when viewed on a mobile device. Read ahead and test your site on mobile. Maybe you can change the theme to make it responsive. Maybe not.

Hopefully, you can make some quick copy tweaks to your website to make it more effective. Then take a fresh look at what you want to accomplish with your website and how you want your new website to look and function. You need to tune into WII-FMc, "What's in it for my clients?"

Today's reality is that every website is outdated every three years. Or less.

Test Your Website

At least monthly you should visit every main page of your website. You don't have to visit every single blog post or product page. You should visit enough pages and posts, however, to know that the website and its links are functioning. You are responsible for everything in your company. This includes your website. Never assume that your website is working. Things break.

Put yourself in the shoes of a first-time visitor. Buy something using your shopping cart. Look for ways to make it easier. Ask a relative to buy something from your website. Watch them go through the buying process. Do they get stuck? Don't offer any help. You want to learn what first-time buyers experience. Most will abandon your shopping cart. You can't blame Amazon for this. You must make sure your buying process works well and is easy to complete.

If your website doesn't help you sell, you won't just lose this one sale. You lose the lifetime value of this client. You also lose the lifetime value of other people who won't hear about your products and services because they've been warned about a horrible online shopping experience. Ouch. Don't let this happen to you.

You need to be a mystery shopper at your website and use your laptop, tablet, and smartphone. That's how your clients and prospects will view your website. Mac and Windows. Android and iPhone. Chrome, Firefox, and Safari. You must know if your website isn't working well so you can fix it. Otherwise, prospects will click away and never call or visit again. You can also delegate this to employees or your spouse. Get their feedback, and use it to make your website better.

Monitoring your website is especially important if you delegate website creation and maintenance to a techie, either an employee or outsourced. Techies generally don't read marketing books and are tone deaf to website hurdles which baffle non-technical website visitors. You expect way too much if you think they will look at things with a marketing mindset.

You can test your website loading speed for Chrome and other browsers here: https://www.webpagetest.org/

You can test your website for mobile-friendliness here: https://search.google.com/test/mobile-friendly.

Website Backup, Updates, and Recovery

Your website is the online foundation of your marketing program. As the business owner, you're responsible for everything in your company, and that includes your website. We've already touched on keeping your website up-to-date, easy-to-use, and marketing-focused. You also need to keep your website safe.

You keep your website safe by protecting it from hackers, keeping the underlying software updated, and backing up everything in case of problems. This is simple if you use a website builder platform such as Squarespace or Weebly. In general, you trust these platforms to protect and back up your website. This is a major reason for paying a little more and using a major website builder platform. These companies know how important this is for their clients and their reputation.

You need to have the following covered to have a safe and secure website. You may do this yourself, or you may farm it out.

Backup and Recovery. A backup copy of your website lets you go back in time and recover your website. This is critical if your website gets hacked and vandalized. Multiple backups are best.

Website Builder: Generally, a nightly backup is performed. Call tech support and ask for a link to an article which explains the backup process.

WordPress: Your website should be backed up by your hosting company. Ask them to be sure. You should also add a backup plug-in, such as DropBox.com, and save your backups to your cloud storage site.

Protection Against Hackers. Bad guys and their bots continuously prowl the web looking for an easy target. Don't let it be you. First, never use "admin" as your website username. Instead, use something scrambled like "eis%698s#0" which can't be guessed. Second, use gibberish for your password such as "diw[45V-1eei9xq#" not "123456" or "monkey." Third, use a password manager like LastPass.com to generate and store strong yet impossible-to-remember usernames and passwords.

Website Builder: Call up technical support and ask for a link to an article explaining what they do to protect against hackers.

WordPress: I install the free version of the WordFence plugin on all my WordPress websites. wordpress.org/plugins/wordfence/

Website Software Updates. Software developers improve their software to add features, improve speed, and fix bugs. My practice is to keep software updated but never be a beta tester. Let others find the bugs.

Website Builder: Nothing for you to install. Everything is kept up-to-date by the company. This is a key advantage for website builder platforms.

WordPress: You have two choices for hosting accounts. Traditional cPanel hosting accounts let you create different types of websites including WordPress. You install WordPress, then install a theme and plugins. You need to keep this updated. I use a plugin called "Automatic Plugin Updates" to keep plugins current. WordPress is set to update automatically. I have to keep the theme updated. None of this is particularly tricky. Just a bother when you have multiple websites.

You'll probably have only one or two websites. You may want WordPress for its power and flexibility. In this case, you should choose a WordPress Hosting solution. With this hosting option, WordPress is pre-installed along with other backup and security plugins.

☐ **ACTION STEP 1:** If you don't have a website, plan your website as discussed in this chapter. Don't neglect Action Steps 2 and 3 during this process. Already have a website? Complete Action Steps 2 and 3.

☐ **ACTION STEP 2:** Learn how your website is being backed up. Contact your website developer and have him prove that your website is being backed up. You can also contact your host company to confirm it performs a nightly backup. You should also save a local copy to your computer or DropBox just in case.

☐ **ACTION STEP 3:** "I'm sorry to report that your sole proprietor website developer was hit by a cement truck today and died at the scene of the accident."

Do you have the usernames and passwords to your domain registrar, hosting company, website dashboard, and any purchased plugins for your website? Do you own your domain name, so you can renew it before it expires? Does your dearly departed website developer own your domain name? Better come up with an action plan for this scenario. Now.

Chapter 48

Create Your Marketing Planner

If you fail to plan, you are planning to fail!
—Benjamin Franklin

Having a large list of clients and hot prospects does you no good if you don't mail your list with news and offers. This chapter is about planning to stay in touch with your clients.

How many times a year do you get in touch with your clients? Quarterly, annually, or only when someone calls you with a question?

Some financial professionals help clients solve a problem and never contact them again. I met with a financial advisor (not my client) who specialized in selling indexed annuities. He would make the sale, fund the annuity, get his commission, and then mark the file for a "call back in 7 years."

Not only does this type of advisor do a disservice to his clients, he also does a disservice to his company. How? Because clients' situations change, and their financial plan or investments need to change. They might inherit money which needs to be invested. This is true for every profession. People have life changes. If you're out of touch, how will you know this? When you forget about them, they're likely to forget about you.

What about your prospects? How often do you get in touch with them? The honest answer for most businesses is "Not often enough."

Let's say someone is referred to you. Do you make three phone calls, leave messages, and promptly forget about them? How often do your clients hear from you? Not so much? Well, you have lots of room for improvement.

100 Client Contacts Per Year

80/20 Tip: I want you to set a goal to get in touch with your 20% Clients and hot prospects 100 times per year. Is this possible? Yes! So where do you start?

You use a planner to track client appointments. You also need a planner to plan and track your marketing activities. I've included a simple marketing planner with the book bonuses.

Do you think 100 touches per year is completely unrealistic? Would this take you away from more important tasks like client meetings? You can do it. Take a look at the following chart. While created for a financial advisor, you can adapt it to your business.

Contact Method	When To Contact	Contacts
Greeting cards	Birthday, Anniversary, 4th of July, and Christmas	4
Newsletter (printed)	Monthly	12
News Update Email	Weekly	52
Holiday Emails	A week before holidays	8
Client letters	Annual review meeting & updates	3
Invitation	Client Appreciation Dinner	1
Invitation	Various seminars and events	6
E-newsletter	Email with various articles	12
Phone call	Random acts of interest	6
TOTAL		100

Following this schedule, you can "touch" your clients 100 times per year. Guess how many of your competitors do this? Probably none. What would happen if you "touched" your prospects just 70 or 80 times a year? Your competitors' best clients would eventually become your clients.

Once set up, you can delegate or automate most of these activities. Your time can be better spent calling up clients with interesting news. For instance, you call your 20% Clients to discuss a recent event in your industry. You call your diehard Los Angeles Lakers fan clients after the Lakers win an NBA championship. Not this year. Maybe next year.

Your business will really begin to grow when you hire and train an assistant. Your assistant can add all new clients and prospects to the email list and the newsletter list. He stacks birthday cards on your desk to be signed. Remember, you can sign a month's worth at a time, and your assistant simply mails them out the week before the big day.

Each touch by itself is small. Individually important? Not really. Urgent? Not unless it's your anniversary or your wife's birthday! Yet taken together, these touches keep you in front of your clients. When they come into some money or have a question, who will they call? You. Moreover, if one of your prospects feels neglected by their provider, who will they call? Again, you.

Depending on your industry, you may have to contact a high-value prospect for years before they become a client. Jim Cecil says it takes an average of 47 months for a high-net-worth investor to change advisors. He calls this "drip marketing" because you nurture prospects into clients with helpful articles, letters, and e-zines over many months. Drip marketing needs to be long-term and automated. You need to be very patient. NurtureMarketing.com

Let me summarize by saying that if your clients feel special, they will most likely remain your clients for a very long time. If you make your prospects feel special, many will become your clients someday. And as your business grows in clients, sales, and profits, you'll feel special.

ACTION STEP: Create a marketing planner for your business and follow it.

Chapter 49

Greeting Cards

The history of greeting cards dates back to the ancient
Chinese who exchanged messages of goodwill to
celebrate a New Year, and to early Egyptians who used
papyrus scrolls to send greetings.
—Greeting Card Association, greetingcard.org

When I get a financial advisor as a consulting client, I tell him to start
mailing a birthday card to every client. Everyone wants to be
remembered on their birthday so sending birthday cards to your
clients should be a no-brainer.

You don't need a USP to do this. You don't need a fresh, engaging,
and persuasive website. You don't need any marketing materials. All
you need is your client database sorted by birthdate, a pile of birthday
cards, a pen, and some stamps. Ideally, your assistant will address the
envelopes and put the cards in front of you for your signature and a
brief note. And it's done.

Financial advisors are hindered by securities compliance
regulations which eliminate many marketing techniques. However,
financial advisors have a legitimate reason to ask for birthdates, so
don't miss this opportunity to make a splash.

What if today's the big day, and you forgot to send a birthday card?
Just give them a call and wish them a happy birthday. I heard Jim
Cecil (nurturemarketing.com) tell the story of an advisor who called a
prospect on her birthday and sang "Happy Birthday" to her. She
almost cried. Why? He was the only person who remembered her
birthday. She asked him if he could trade securities. He said "Yes!"
and got a million-dollar trade that day. Now he knows how to sing
"Happy Birthday" in six languages!

Anniversaries are another great time to send a card. You'll stand out by remembering a special day. A twist on the anniversary card is to call the husband two weeks before the anniversary to remind him of the big day. Beyond saving a client, you might save a marriage!

You can also send greeting cards to clients and prospects on other important days of the year. Christmas cards should go out early in December, so your card will stand out. Getting too close to Christmas? Send a New Year's Day card out between Christmas and New Years and wish them prosperity in the new year.

Another good time to send a greeting card would be Independence Day, better known in the U.S. as the 4th of July. Finally, have a supply of "Get Well Soon" cards so you can send one out whenever you call a client and learn they are sick.

In this day of email overload, your cards help you stand out and be remembered by your clients. Everyone enjoys getting birthday cards, Christmas cards, and "Get Well Soon" cards.

Do you have to send them to all your clients and prospects? No, but you might start sending birthday cards to your top 100 clients and expand your mailing over time.

Buy some cards today and get ready to send them out. Best practice is a hand-addressed envelope with a postage stamp. However, if you need to use mailing labels and a postage meter, that's okay too. The main thing is to get it done, get it out there, and get noticed by your clients.

You can also send out cards using an online service. Not as personal but a lot more efficient. Here are three services to consider.

AmazingMail.com

Click2mail.com/by-product/notecards

Sendoutcards.com/business

ACTION STEP: Buy a box of greeting cards and some stamps. Get ready to wow someone. Then do it.

Chapter 50

Emails Are Sales Letters

"You've Got Mail."
—Romantic comedy starring Tom Hanks and Meg Ryan

To my younger readers, it must seem insane that people used to look forward to checking their email. Getting email was a big deal. The America Online email client announced "You've got mail!" as if it were Christmas morning. A 1998 movie about email pen pals and local bookstores grossed $250 million. Someone should produce a dark sequel and call it "You've Got Spam."

In today's world, you need to view every client email as a marketing piece. Whether a quick email to a client or your client e-newsletter, treat your emails as advertisements and you'll get more bang for your buck. I realize that email is free, but your client's time is not. Never waste it and never bore a client.

With practice, you'll write your emails as persuasive mini-advertisements. Remember that your emails may get forwarded to a friend of a 20% client. You want to make a great first impression. Even with email.

Here is the advertisement structure for email:

- Subject line (which is the headline)
- Message body
- Call to Action
- Contact information

Let's take a closer look at each part to maximize the marketing impact.

Subject Line. To get your email opened and read you need a powerful subject line. Copywriter and author Mark Ford (aka Michael Masterson) created the "4 U Formula" to get his emails opened and read: Subject lines should be urgent, useful, unique, and ultra-specific. How would this formula be used for an estate planning attorney? Let's imagine he's putting on a living trust seminar. He has created wills for thousands of people over the years. He wants them to come to his seminar to learn about living trusts.

Subject: "Can your will protect your assets? Learn if you need a trust this Tuesday evening."

Does this subject line hit all four U's?

Urgent: "... this Tuesday evening" Yes

Useful: "... protect your assets" Yes

Unique: " ... your will ... " Okay.

Ultra-specific: "Learn if you need a living trust" Yes

When you use this formula, rate your subject line for each of these four areas. Don't be generic or spammy. Be helpful. Speak to your avatar.

Well-crafted subject lines let your client know the importance of a particular message immediately. Compare specific subject lines to "Hey, there!" or "article to read" or even worse, the blank subject line.

Message Body. After a personal greeting ("Hello, Bob") get to the point quickly, and keep it brief. You're staying in touch and don't need to elaborate. I try to use proper English and avoid trendy shortcuts like "lol" or "otfl" used in texting. You never want your client to feel stupid if they don't know you're saying, "laugh out loud" or "on the floor laughing." I speak from experience. For several years I thought "lol" meant "lots of luck." Who knew? I didn't. The same thing goes for jargon. Avoid jargon as much as possible. Define terms when you use industry jargon.

Call to Action. You need to tell or suggest something for your client to do at the end of the email. You might say, "I hope to see you at the seminar. Feel free to bring a friend." Or "Call me after you read this article. I have some ideas on how to apply this to your situation."

Contact Information. Always use an email signature which includes your name, title, company name, address, phone number, email address, and website. Make it easy for the person to get back in touch with you.

Don't overdo these personal emails, or your client may think you're spamming them. These are supposed to be personal one-to-one emails, which are different from the one-to-many emails we'll discuss in the next chapter.

Direct mail trivia: America Online grew rapidly using direct mail to send tens of millions of installation disks to potential subscribers. At one point in 1993, 50% of the CDs produced worldwide bore an AOL logo. By 1997, about half of all U.S. homes with Internet access had it through AOL. The movie "You've Got Mail" came out the next year. Source: wikipedia.org/wiki/AOL.

ACTION STEP: If you don't have an email list, start one with the emails in your inbox. Send an email using the formula above. Rinse and repeat.

Chapter 51

Email Marketing

> The only wrong thing to do in email is be boring. Some topics are inherently more serious than others, so fun may not be exactly what you want to do. In those cases make sure you're at least interesting.
>
> —Ben Settle

Email marketing lets you stay in touch with your clients and prospects on a daily, weekly, or monthly basis, or whenever you have something interesting to share. You can send an e-newsletter with several articles or an email highlighting one important topic. You include links to your website for more information or to make a purchase. And, unlike most other forms of advertising, email is free.

Email marketing refers to sending your message to part or all of your client and prospect lists via email. Sometimes you send your message to both clients and prospects. This could be your monthly e-newsletter or a store-wide sale announcement. Other times you'll send information to clients only. You can also segment your list and send specific messages to specific groups of clients. You can send special offers to your prospects to help them make that first purchase from you. **80/20 Tip:** You can send extra emails to your 20% Clients for special offers or invitation-only events.

You may already have email addresses for your clients and prospects. If not, you need to start collecting them for future use. Be sure to ask visitors to join your email list on your website and other client communications. Your goal is to collect as many email addresses as you can. On platforms such as Facebook and Twitter, you don't have full control over your list of followers. These companies can and will change the rules without notice. You control and own your email list, so building an email list should be a top priority.

Create a spreadsheet and enter all the email addresses you have. Add new email addresses as you get them. Later you'll be able to upload these email addresses into your e-newsletter program and save a lot of data entry time.

A monthly email newsletter can contain articles of interest on current news plus timeless articles on best practices in your industry. You want to include a personal message from you to say hello and make a comment relating to the season of the year.

Financial professionals can also send a weekly economic update which shares market information and economic analysis. Other than a personal message, financial advisors won't write any of this. You need compliant, timely information, created by someone else such as Peter Montoya's Marketing Library. CPAs can send out tax tips and updates on state and federal tax law changes. Real estate agents, carpet cleaners, home security companies, and other local businesses can send information to homeowners about how to improve and enjoy your home.

You can save a lot of time by using an industry-specific email platform. For example, BroadRidge.com does email and print newsletters in several industries including consumer finance, healthcare, insurance, retail banking, telecom, and utilities. Financial professionals need pre-approved, compliant, timely, and interesting articles. Otherwise, you'll spend too much time dealing with your compliance department. You should find a platform you like and ask for some sample e-newsletters to see what they look like from your clients' perspective. You'll stay in touch without having to write the content. (You can also get information about their print newsletters, which we cover next in Chapter 52.)

You can send out your emails using general purpose email systems such as Mailchimp, AWeber, and ConvertKit. These companies let you build an email list and broadcast email newsletters and updates to all or segments of your mailing list. You can set up autoresponders to send new subscribers a series of introductory messages. Your Customer Relationship Management (CRM) software may also have this capability.

How Often Should I Email?

Should you email your list daily, weekly, monthly, or whenever you feel like it? This depends on your client base and your prospect target list. I would not appreciate a daily email from the realtor who helped me buy my last home if all he wrote about was buying and selling real estate. I would quickly unsubscribe, because I don't buy or sell real estate very often. However, I do look forward to a monthly real estate update from another broker because it contains area statistics on listings, average sales values, and sales volume. A daily email from a real estate agent would need to include home improvement ideas and ways to enjoy my home—and never be boring. If you can offer daily deals to your hungry client list, send a daily update with time-limited offers. Whatever you do, be consistent, so your audience knows what to expect both on timing and content.

Keep It Personal

You should include your name and contact information in every edition of your e-zine. You must make it easy for clients and prospects to reach you with comments and questions regarding the articles. This also makes it easy for them to refer you to their friends.

There are several ways to make your emails more personal. First, put your name or an employee's name in the "From:" box and not the name of your company. Next, avoid big graphical headers and send plain text emails. Plain text emails look less salesy and generally get a better response these days. Because of email spam and malware attacks, many people will read your emails as plain text regardless of your formatting. Plain text emails are less work to put together. Of course, opinions vary on this, and many successful email marketers have a full-color header and HTML formatted messages. You should end your emails with your name, as if you were sending an email to a friend. Finally, always send yourself a test email before mailing your list.

Using Autoresponders

You can use an autoresponder to send a series of emails to new subscribers. This can be a series of how-to-get-started messages covering the fundamentals of your business area. For example, a CPA might have a series of ten emails covering the ten most common tax mistakes and why homeowners and business owners should care.

Notice I didn't write, "the top ten tax mistakes and how to avoid them." In general, you tell them about a problem and why they should be concerned. To learn how to solve the problem, they need to contact you or buy your service or product. In other words, the "what" and "why" are free, but the "how-to" costs money. Otherwise, why click the link or call you up?

Finally, you must keep it fresh and interesting. If your email is boring, they won't read it at all. They'll click "unsubscribe," and they're off your list.

Email newsletters are cheap, easy, and very efficient, but not enough to replace all printed communications. They're also no replacement for phone calls and other forms of personal contact.

☐ **ACTION STEP: Do you have a client email list? If not, start building it today. If you have a list, segment your 20% Clients for special offer emails.**

Chapter 52

Print Newsletters

Print newsletters arriving by mail, opened, physically handled, read, clipped from, saved, and shared have positive effects that *cannot* be replicated online.

—Dan Kennedy

Email is free. And everyone's doing it. Take a look at your inbox. Clogged with messages? Do you read them all? Be honest. We all suffer from email overload these days. Dare to be different. Stand out from the crowd with an interesting, easy-to-read, and timely print newsletter mailed to your clients and better prospects.

The collapse in first-class and standard mail is tough on the U.S. Postal Service. Blame email and electronic bill payment. However, less mail in your client's mailbox mean your letters, postcards, and newsletters really stand out.

A printed newsletter will keep you in front of your clients and give them something interesting to read away from the computer. You may use purchased industry-related content or create custom content for your newsletter. You don't need to do this work yourself. You can have an employee or virtual assistant write articles on topics you select.

Your newsletter should display your USP in the masthead. Articles can elaborate on your USP and elevator pitch. You'll educate your readers about who you help and what sets you apart.

Wondering what to write about? Here are 12 ideas to get you started.

1. Case studies about how a client used your products and services.

2. How you or an employee help make your community a better place.

3. Current events in your community and how they impact your clients.

4. Something humorous about your industry. Or just clean, random jokes.

5. You can highlight one product or service per month. Focus on benefits.

6. Introduce new products and services. Promote with a coupon.

7. Testimonials from satisfied clients.

8. Something related to the next holiday.

9. Tips in your area of expertise.

10. Answer a common question. Ask for questions to be answered.

11. Industry news your clients might find interesting

12. "Referral of the Month" story about how a client referral lead to helping someone in need of your products and services.

Every newsletter should have at least one call to action to motivate clients to do something. This could be to call your office to make a purchase or get answers to questions, visit your website to buy something or get more information, or mark their calendars for an upcoming event.

Your staff must be trained to keep your mailing list up-to-date with current mailing addresses for all clients and prospects.

Should you mail first class or standard rate postage? This depends on your business. First class mail costs more but has a much higher delivery rate. With first-class mail, the post office notifies you of address changes when you put the phrase "address service requested" somewhere on the envelope. Have a huge list? You can clean your list by mailing first class once a year, and use standard postage the rest of the time.

The newsletter goes out automatically on the schedule you set. You can mail it out monthly or quarterly. You can choose to send it to all your clients and prospects or your clients and only A-List prospects. This depends on how many people you have on your mailing list and the size of your budget.

A printed newsletter is an ideal vehicle for staying in touch with qualified prospects you meet at community seminars and website visitors who leave additional contact information. These are prospects who already know something about you and your expertise. You can follow up with your hot prospects by calling them a week after the newsletter gets mailed. Ask if they received it and have any questions.

Don't over complicate this. Once a year, I get a printed two-page market update from a local mortgage broker. He prints it on his company letterhead. He includes a business card. I used him to finance my house several years ago. His brief yet interesting print newsletter keeps him in touch with me at a low cost. I'm much more likely to remember him when I buy another piece of real estate—and when a friend asks for a great place to get a mortgage.

> **ACTION STEP: Consider a printed newsletter for your 20% Clients. Keep newsletters you receive to get ideas for your newsletter.**

Chapter 53

Client Letters Are Sales Letters

> Your challenge and your biggest opportunity, if you're going to retain and sustain significant client transactions, is to keep those clients constantly connected to you.
>
> —Jay Abraham, *Getting Everything You Can Out of All You've Got*

Whenever you communicate with a client, you send a multi-layered message. You're not simply sending a reminder of a meeting. Every client letter is a "touch" and should be written as a sales letter.

Your client letters should be low key, friendly, and never scream at a client like a Publishers Clearing House Sweepstakes mailer. Let's imagine Natalie is already your client. You don't need to use giant headlines with big promises to catch her attention.

Instead, you project your image as a business professional. You avoid industry jargon to avoid making Natalie feel stupid. You state things in an interesting and plain-English manner. You are reminding her that she made a wise choice by retaining you and not one of your competitors.

Your letterhead should include all your contact information in a large, easy-to-read font. Include your USP to remind them of what sets you apart from everyone else.

Every letter follows the basic pattern of every effective advertisement. Let's look at the components:

Headline: The opening paragraph can be a single sentence which states the purpose of the letter.

Body: The next couple paragraphs expand on the purpose of the letter and include details to keep the client reading and prime them for action. Brevity and clarity are key here.

Offer and Call to Action: This will vary widely depending on the purpose of the letter. You must provide the reader with a clear idea of what you want them to do. "Remember to bring your last three years' tax returns (Form 1040 only), and I'll see you on Tuesday at 10 am."

You can also end with a P.S. to boost your main message. After the opening paragraph, the P.S. is the most read part of any sales letter. Example: "P.S. If you have any questions before our meeting, please give me a call at 222-333-4444."

Let's look briefly at different types of client letters.

Initial Meetings

You've spent good money getting a prospect to attend your seminar or to read one of your advertisements. The prospect calls to set an appointment. Now you're following up with a letter to confirm all the details. You need to make a strong first impression with this letter, or else they might not even show up.

You or your assistant should begin with your standard letter. Much of the who, what, when, where, why, and how of this letter will be the same. Your letter will pack an extra punch if you can reference one personal detail about the person or couple. If you learn something about them at a living trust seminar, jot it down on the back of the evaluation. Your assistant might find something out during a call to set the appointment. Remember that you're starting a relationship with a person. Don't be afraid to get a little personal.

A well-crafted client letter reminds your client why you are meeting, what to bring to the meeting, and the date and time of the meeting.

Event Announcements

When you promote an event, it's a good practice to include a cover letter along with a flyer. Both will contain much of the same information. Some people will carefully read the letter, while others will toss the letter and put the flyer on their refrigerator door.

You want folks who already know you, like you, and trust you to help you promote your event.

For client appreciation dinners, you may want your clients to bring two guests. In that case, you should include two flyers and say, "Here's an extra flyer for a friend."

For community seminars, it's okay to send a letter to clients who already have a living trust or long-term care insurance. Your letter can remind them they made a smart decision to protect their spouses and heirs with a living trust. Then ask them to pass on the flyer to a neighbor who could benefit from this information.

Post-Purchase Letters

Everyone suffers from buyer's remorse now and then. Sometimes that leads to an order cancellation or delay, and you're back in the sales mode again. You can reduce that possibility when you send a post-purchase letter or email.

Your post-purchase letter restates your offer and reassures them that they made the right decision. This letter or email is especially important after an initial purchase. You remind them why your company was their best choice. Help them imagine the results. You show that you appreciate their business and will work hard to keep it in the future. You remind them of your guarantee, so there really is no risk. You tell them how to get back in touch with you whenever they have any additional questions. You can also remind them of the next step in the service or product delivery process.

The worst time for a client to feel neglected is immediately after becoming a client. That's why a post-purchase letter is so important.

Article Clipping

You'll make points with your clients if you send them articles of interest. If a person enjoys power boating, send them an article on new water toys. If they have lots of commercial real estate, send them an article on market trends.

You don't even need to draft a letter. Just attach a 3x3 Post-it note with "Bob, FYI. Bill."

Article clipping takes a little time but pays big dividends over time. You neglect clients at your peril. Sending an article once in a while makes you stand out.

ACTION STEP: In your pile of current and past ads, did you include your client form letters? Review your client letters now and turn them into sales letters.

Chapter 54

Client Appreciation Dinners

> Appreciate everything your associates do for the
> business. Nothing else can quite substitute for a few
> well-chosen, well-timed, sincere words of praise. They're
> absolutely free and worth a fortune.
>
> —Sam Walton

Feeling neglected is the #1 reason people leave one company for another. Not price. Not service quality. Not product features. Instead, everyone wants to feel appreciated and remembered. Especially clients who spend a considerable amount of money in your business each year. When you host an annual client appreciation dinner, your clients feel appreciated and are reminded why they do business with you.

I recommend a client meal. This can be a luncheon or a dinner. Nothing says "Thank you!" like a meal. I recommend dinners. This works best when you serve high net worth individuals. You can afford to show your appreciation.

80/20 Tip: Client appreciation dinners help you build your business by attracting more 20% Clients to a positive, non-salesy, and fun event. Your invitation should encourage your clients to bring another couple with them to enjoy the evening. Generally speaking, people's social circles usually include people of similar economic status. People who live in expensive neighborhoods have neighbors who need a qualified professional. Like you. You leverage your time by building chemistry with lots of folks at the same time.

During the event, schedule time for people to say kind words about you. You tell a few close, trusted clients about this ahead of time, so they come prepared to wax eloquent about you. Others will get the idea, and you'll be praised (and a little bit roasted) by people who appreciate what you've done for them. You'll get results-oriented testimonials heard by friends of clients. While personal testimonials aren't allowed on your website if you're a financial advisor, even somewhat "canned" affirmations are credible and helpful to get new clients. For most other businesses, you can transcribe and edit these testimonials, get permission to use the quote, and add them to your website and other marketing materials.

When should you hold this event? This depends on where you live and who your targeted clientele is. However, there are two times you can count on. You can host a BBQ for families during the summer or a sit-down couple's dinner in December.

You want to make the event great and worth the time of your clients and their friends, so don't go cheap on the food or the venue. You only have one chance to make a good first impression with your prospective clients. Make it memorable.

Consider having a well-known guest speaker for the event—one you can trust to be in top form. Limit the talk to about 15 minutes, because it is a party after all. Be sure to encourage your guests to speak personally with your featured guest during the event.

Your event could follow a program like this:

- You welcome everyone and express your appreciation.

- Dinner is served.

- Your guest speaker talks during dessert.

- Words of appreciation by your clients.

- You express your outlook on the upcoming year.

- Informal social time to meet one another and chat with the guest speaker.

When you hold a client appreciation dinner in December, thank your clients for their business, make them feel appreciated, and connect with their friends and relatives. Do it right, and you'll have a very busy January and February!

Does it have to be so formal and be a full meal? No. I manage a commercial office building, and we celebrated five years with a BBQ cookout. (Based on your outdoor space, consider bringing a mic and speakers.) We rented a huge tent and had a full-blown luncheon in the parking lot. It was a hit!

Our office complex is 100% leased now, so we can't block off a big chunk of the parking lot for anything during business hours. For the tenth anniversary, we had a local ice cream truck roll into the parking lot at 1 pm. We sent out invitations which looked like something between an invitation and a coupon; each invitation was worth one ice cream treat. The ice cream truck was also a big hit. Everyone felt appreciated, and now it's an annual tradition.

☐ **ACTION STEP: How can you use a client dinner or other food treat to make your 20% Clients feel special this year?**

Chapter 55

Client Meetings Are Sales Meetings

You're always selling.

—Joseph Morabito

Why write about client meetings in a marketing book? Because you want to grow your business. Effective marketing must be followed by effective selling. Otherwise, you'll fill your office or store with qualified prospects who never become revenue-generating clients.

People ask me all the time, "What's the difference between sales and marketing?" I tell them, "Marketing is leading a horse to water. Sales is persuading the horse to drink."

Of course, you're selling whenever you're speaking to prospects. This includes community seminars, radio shows, or getting quoted in your local newspaper after you send out a press release. People are getting to know you, like you, and trust you. Never forget that you're selling yourself every time you open your mouth.

Yet it's in your office or store where the selling really happens. You'll either begin cementing a relationship or cause it to hit the rocks before it even gets going.

Let's look at some ways to increase your closing ratio.

Listen to Dale Carnegie

Dale Carnegie wrote one of the best-selling business books of all time, *How to Win Friends and Influence People.*

> So if you aspire to be a good conversationalist, be an attentive listener. To be interesting, be interested. Ask questions that other persons will enjoy answering. Encourage them to talk about themselves and their accomplishments. Remember that the people you are talking to are a hundred times more interested in themselves and their wants and problems than they are in you

and your problems. A person's toothache means more to that person than a famine in China which kills a million people.... Think of that the next time you start a conversation.

A client once told me about a financial advisor he knew from college. The advisor used community seminars to get prospects into his office. However, he seldom closed business because he saw himself as an "educator." He was the professor, and his prospects were his students. He showed them how much he knew by overloading them with his investment knowledge. Unfortunately, his students skipped class and found another teacher, i.e., advisor.

God made us with two ears and one mouth. Remember this ratio, and you'll let your prospects do the majority of the talking. You'll find it easier to watch body language while listening. If the person sits back in their chair, you need to keep building rapport. If the person is on the edge of his seat and pushing their personal information in your direction, he wants to hear what you think now.

Be Ready for Difficult Questions

Financial advisors ask clients pointed and personal questions, such as, "What's your tolerance for risk?" "Are you okay with short-term losses to make long-term gains?" And, "Who gets your money when you die?"

Sometimes clients have ready answers. Other times a couple will look at each other blankly and say, "We need to talk about this." No problem, you don't expect a ready answer to every tough question.

However, what about when your client or a prospective client asks YOU some tough questions? Are you ready with good answers?

Fortune magazine named Steve Jobs the "CEO of the Decade" in 2009. The article said, "A key Jobs business tool is his mastery of the message. He rehearses over and over every line he and others utter in public about Apple."

In most cases, you'll meet with your client in your office. A larger venue might be a community seminar with 25 or 30 people. Your ability to provide a sincere and convincing answer can determine whether you win or lose the account.

Here are some difficult questions for financial advisors:

- Why are you a financial advisor?

- How do you get paid on this investment?

- Do you put your recommendations in writing?

- How do you invest your own money?

That last question might stump many advisors. Other professionals will face similar questions. Would you use a realtor to buy a house who has rented his whole life? Or buy stocks through a stockbroker who keeps all his money in money market funds? Would you trust your savings with a banker who keeps his savings under his mattress? Probably not. Of course, your season in life could be entirely different from that of your prospect. You need to be ready for these types of questions.

You need to develop clear, convincing, and sincere answers to these types of questions. Practice in front of a mirror. Ask your spouse to role-play. Or use your webcam to record your answers, and give them a critical view. You'll be glad you did. You'll keep the selling process going, build trust, and close more business.

Ask for Referrals

When a meeting goes well, ask for referrals. This is especially true when you're meeting with one of your 20% Clients. You can honestly tell them that "by getting referrals from people like you, I can spend less money on advertising, spend more money on serving clients, and still grow my business."

80/20 Tip: By asking for referrals, you're selling your 20% Clients on why their friends should do business with you. You are uniquely qualified to serve them, you stay connected with them, and make them feel important. Why wouldn't they give you quality referrals?

ACTION STEP: Get out your appointment calendar. Write "SELL" at the top of the page. This will remind you to sell and not just chit-chat.

Review of Part 4

"Reach Out and Touch Someone."
—AT&T 1980s advertising campaign

You may not like picking up the phone and chatting with clients. You might not like sending out daily or weekly emails to inform, amuse, and sell. You might not enjoy spending hours to update your seven-year-old website. However, connecting with your clients is always more fun than receiving bills from advertisers.

In this section, we looked at lots of ways to stay connected with your clients. We began by looking at what happens when you neglect your clients: They become your competitors' clients. When you lose clients, you need to spend more money on advertising to attract new prospects. Regardless of how wonderful your products and services are, you must make your clients feel appreciated. I keep repeating myself because appreciation is so important.

You now know that client referral systems will turbocharge your word-of-mouth advertising. The lifetime value of your clients reveals how much you can spend on client acquisition. This includes referral incentives, client retention efforts, and of course, advertising. You also learned ways to get inactive clients back and buying again.

The rest of this section covered specific tactics to stay connected with your clients. We began with your website, which serves the dual purpose of advertising your business to prospects and serving your existing clients. You really do own your website, unlike your Facebook business page or LinkedIn profile. You control how your website looks and functions.

Your marketing plan is your roadmap to staying connected with your clients throughout the year. The rest of this section covered greeting cards, email, newsletters, client letters, client appreciation dinners, and client meetings. You know lots of ways to stay connected, stay in the mind of your clients, and offer them ways to get what they want in life by buying it from you.

I'll summarize each chapter of Part 4 into a single sentence:

Chapter 41: You serve your clients well when you keep them informed and offer them special deals which meet their needs.

Chapter 42: You know your clients well when you know all about them, including what they buy and why they buy, and have this information in a client list.

Chapter 43: Your referral systems give you an enthusiastic and unpaid sales force.

Chapter 44: You must know the lifetime value of your clients to know how much you can invest to get a new client.

Chapter 45: The easiest way to grow any business is to reconnect with inactive clients.

Chapter 46: You own your website, so make it great.

Chapter 47: If your website isn't great, do a website makeover.

Chapter 48: If you fail to plan your client communications, you plan to fail.

Chapter 49: Greeting cards are low tech, inexpensive, and proven to please.

Chapter 50: Client emails are mini-sales letters and should never be boring.

Chapter 51: Client e-newsletters keep you connected with your clients.

Chapter 52: Print newsletters help you stand apart from your competitors.

Chapter 53: Client letters are sales letters, not form letters.

Chapter 54: Client appreciation dinners demonstrate your appreciation for your clients and provide a great way to get testimonials.

Chapter 55: Use client meetings to learn what your clients want and show them how to get it.

Conclusion

You've reached the end of this book and have begun your journey as your own marketing consultant. Now you get to implement what you've learned. Many marketing activities will pay you dividends for years. Other marketing activities will shift as your marketplace changes and advertising platforms come and go. That's okay. You now know time-tested and timeless marketing principles to grow your business and leave your competitors in the dust.

Let's review what you've learned:

In Part 1, you learned that marketing must be a key focus for you as the business owner. That takes time and energy. Your payoff is a growing business with predictable ways to get new clients and sell more to existing clients.

In Parts 2, 3, and 4, we covered the three ways to grow any business. Let's review the growth formula we studied in Chapter 2.

1. Get More Clients. You attract more prospects and convert a higher percentage of prospects into clients. We covered how to do this in Part 3: Get Noticed. You learned how to create effective ads with better copywriting and graphic design. You also learned how to get new clients using endorsement letters in Chapter 21.

2. Increase Your Average Sale. McDonald's increased sales of fries 15% by simply asking, "Do you want fries with that?" We covered how to do this in Part 2: Be Unique. Yes, creating a USP for your business is a lot of work. However, you'll probably only need to do it once, and then you'll reap the rewards for years to come.

Being perceived as unique in your marketplace sets you apart from your competitors, makes it easier for your clients to make referrals, and makes it easier to get other professionals to endorse you over anyone else. You are no longer a commodity.

3. Increase the Frequency of Repurchase. You want your clients to buy from you more often. McDonald's added the Egg McMuffin and breakfast in 1972; by 1981 breakfast was 18% of sales. Now McDonald's serves breakfast all day long. We covered how to increase repeat business in Part 4: Stay Connected. By staying in touch with your clients, you increase revenues from existing clients and reduce client attrition.

You know the importance of calculating the lifetime value of your clients. You can spend more to get new clients with this knowledge. You can also afford to stay in touch with your clients so they feel wanted (and have more opportunities to spend more money with you.) These three growth factors work together to grow your sales exponentially.

	Current	Year 1
Clients (A)	100	110
Average Sale (B)	$100	$110
Purchases per year (C)	10	11
Annual Sales (A x B x C)	$100,000	$133,100
Sales Growth		33%

Your revenues will grow by 33% when you increase the three growth factors by 10%. You double your revenues by increasing these factors by 26%. Whether it takes one year or two, you can do it.

Read this book again, and complete the action steps one at a time. You don't need to do everything taught in this book to double your business. However, you do need to get going now, because otherwise you'll remain stuck right where you are. Take advantage of the book bonuses, which will help you in this effort.

Don't get hung up by perfectionism. Just get started and improve what you're doing. You can always go back and do it again better. You *should* go back and try to do things better. Also remember that 20% of effort generates 80% of results. For many tasks getting things 80% done will be good enough.

Keep learning about marketing and your market. Test what you're doing and make small improvements to your marketing systems.

These improvements add up over time. Always seek to know and understand your market your avatar better.

You have learned many proven and profitable ways to grow your business. Over time, you'll discover which marketing strategies work best for your business. This takes time to develop. Once in place, you can run your business profitably without worrying about how to get more clients. And you won't waste time wondering if you need to try the latest marketing fad.

Finally, keep doing what works even when you get tired of it. I worked with one estate planning attorney who did nearly 1,000 living trust seminars over a 20-year period. Yet each new batch of seminar attendees saw it for the first time and always learned a lot. And, regardless of how often he's done it, he gets new clients every time. Now you go and do likewise.

For Further Study

Books to Read (and Re-read)

Living the 80/20 Way: Work Less, Worry Less, Succeed More, Enjoy More by Richard Koch. This book will open your eyes to the 80/20 principle and how you can leverage its power in your business and personal life.

Getting Everything You Can Out of All You've Got: 21 Ways You Can Out-Think, Out-Perform, and Out-Earn the Competition by Jay Abraham. You'll learn more about being unique, getting noticed by your prospects, and staying connected with your clients in this insightful book by my first marketing mentor.

The Copywriter's Handbook: A Step-By-Step Guide to Writing Copy That Sells, 3rd Ed., by Robert W. Bly. A modern-day classic and one of my most referenced books on copywriting. Read it and reap.

How to Write a Good Advertisement by Victor Schwab. Written by an A-List copywriter with 44 years of copywriting experience, this classic book has helped thousands of copywriters create effective ads for over 50 years.

The Non-Designer's Design Book, 4th Ed., by Robin Williams. The subtitle says it all: "Design and typographic principles for the visual novice." Trust me, you need this book.

Reality in Advertising by Rosser Reeves. You'll learn more about how to use your unique selling proposition to build your brand and make more sales.

Scientific Advertising by Claude C. Hopkins. A classic book by the father of modern advertising.

Book Bonuses

"But wait, there's more!" I've created some marketing tools to help you implement what you learn in this book. This includes worksheets, checklists, ad templates, and a collection of classic advertisements to study. These tools just won't fit within the confines of a paperback or eBook.

In addition to these tools, I'll stay in touch by emailing business tips, special offers, and more ways to grow your business. You'll also be first to hear about my future books. Get your marketing tools here: richardemmons.com/marketingbonus/

ChamberCrowd.com

Chapter 20 covered how to get noticed without advertising. If you followed the action step, you now belong to your local chamber of commerce. Congratulations. In this case, you are now eligible to join ChamberCrowd, the secure social network for chamber members serious about boosting sales and profits.

I created ChamberCrowd.com to give chamber members a better, non-Facebook place to get answers to business questions, network with other chamber members, and learn additional ways to grow a successful, enjoyable and profitable business.

Your membership in ChamberCrowd includes my free course, Marketing Survival Class, which takes you through the marketing strategies taught in this book. Join other busy business owners and managers who are doing the same thing: investing time to improve marketing while avoiding the daily distractions we all face.

Learn more at www.ChamberCrowd.com

Index

80/20, 19, 20, 31, 35, 43, 108, 112, 127, 132, 176, 197, 203, 207, 234, 243, 255, 261, 269

Abraham, Jay, vii, 5, 6, 7, 49, 73, 84, 97, 101, 120, 181, 189, 194, 195, 199, 201, 204, 205, 251, 269, 275
Ad layout, 152, 168
Ad tracking, 143
Administration, 21, 23
Adobe, 155
Advertising agencies, 96
Advertising budget, 91, 93, 96, 133, 144, 175, 179, 183
Advertising formulas, 119, 120
Advertising tests, 93, 104, 130, 266
Advertising, direct response, 97, 182
Advertising, image, 95, 179
Advertising, online, 171, 175
Advertorial, 164
AIDA, 120
Amazon.com, 39, 47, 51, 77, 153, 161, 214, 219, 228
Apple, 19, 33, 41, 96, 150, 152, 157, 158, 260
AT&T, 263
Attention, 113, 120, 121, 122, 129, 215
Avatar, 104, 107, 116, 132, 135, 149, 156, 171, 182, 192, 212, 217, 240

Bencivenga, Gary, 112
Bing, 210, 217

Biography, 59, 63
Bly, Robert, vii, 57, 59, 95, 97, 129, 147, 269
BNI, Business Networking International, 84
Boardroom Books, 121
Boardroom, The, vii, xiii, 23, 24, 67, 138, 224
Brand, 24, 39, 40, 41, 46, 76, 78, 85, 99, 153, 157, 159, 182, 216, 269
Burger King, 96

Call To Action, 95, 97, 121, 126, 138, 140, 141, 151, 163, 166, 168, 172, 182, 208, 213, 215, 224, 239, 248, 252
Canva.com, 152, 153, 154, 155, 160
Caples, John, 101, 111, 133, 137, 141, 143, 148
Carnegie, Dale, 129, 259
Carpet cleaners, 111, 138, 212, 244
Chamber of Commerce, xiii, 40, 70, 74, 83, 96, 109, 155, 175, 181, 193
Chiropractors, 207
Client database, 191, 208, 237
Client letters, 234, 264
Client list, xviii, 182, 191, 194, 208, 245, 264
Clients, 5, 7, 8, 49, 87, 189, 191, 205, 265
Copy, 61, 66, 82, 102, 104, 107, 111, 113, 115, 124, 129, 141, 147, 149, 152, 163, 168, 170, 215,

220, 223, 224, 227
Copy bullets, 69, 121, 124, 132, 151
Copywriting, vii, xiv, 82, 111, 112, 116, 117, 119, 133, 141, 147, 149, 170, 181, 226, 265
CPAs, 9, 23, 24, 30, 35, 52, 87, 138, 180, 212, 244, 245
CRM, 30, 31, 34, 193, 244
Customers, xv, 5, 19, 35, 39, 46

Demographics, 108
Direct mail, 97, 241
Display ads, 163
Domino's Pizza, 46, 47, 54
Drip marketing, 235
Drucker, Peter, 29, 35
DrudgeReport.com, 216

Easy, 8, 10, 11, 22, 29, 32, 42, 43, 44, 47, 54, 69, 85, 96, 97, 101, 114, 124, 139, 141, 147, 151, 153, 161, 163, 166, 172, 202, 208, 212, 213, 214, 215, 216, 217, 224, 228, 229, 230, 240, 245, 247, 251
Ecommerce, 214
Edison, Thomas, xv
Email, 20, 216, 234, 243, 247
Emmons Sisters band, The, 98
Emmons, Richard, 39, 61, 67, 198, 219, 275
Emotional, 116
Employees, 48, 122, 134
Endorsement letters, 81, 87, 180, 181, 265
Engineers, 138, 212

Facebook, 12, 20, 26, 42, 89, 154, 171, 172, 173, 180, 192, 210, 213, 219, 243, 263
FedEx, 46, 54, 69, 74, 124, 126, 161
Financial advisors, 59, 61, 212, 217, 233, 235, 237, 244, 256, 260
Ford, Mark, vii, 239

Forde, John, 156, 163, 169
Franchise, 39, 40
Free, 134, 139, 155, 169, 210, 213, 226

Garfinkel, David, 141
Gleeck, Fred, 127
Godin, Seth, 157
Goodby, Jeff, 114
Google, xvi, 12, 47, 113, 138, 171, 172, 173, 175, 210, 211, 213, 217, 218, 220
Grants Pass, Oregon, xiii, 67, 69, 139
Graphic design, xiv, 82, 96, 104, 111, 112, 122, 147, 148, 149, 151, 152, 155, 163, 166, 167, 170, 182, 265
Graphic designer, xvi, 81, 112, 147, 148, 149, 155, 156, 157, 158, 160, 161, 163, 169
Greeting cards, 234, 237, 264
Growth factors, 7, 8, 10, 266
Guarantee, 47, 51, 68, 126, 165

Haller, Lori, 149
Hatch, Dennis, 117
Headline, 69, 70, 98, 112, 120, 121, 122, 124, 127, 129, 130, 131, 132, 133, 134, 135, 141, 147, 150, 151, 152, 153, 154, 163, 165, 166, 167, 168, 171, 173, 182, 208, 212, 215, 220, 239, 251
Home Depot, 47, 138
Hopkins, Claude, 91, 92, 269

Images, 69, 111, 114, 143, 147, 152, 159, 169, 216, 224, 227
Insurance agents, 5, 42, 87, 89, 138, 212

Jobs, Steve, 41, 158, 223, 260

KAJO, 123
Kennedy, Dan, 45, 49, 121, 137, 201, 247

Kennedy, John E., 112

Landing pages, 213
Lawyers, 5, 42, 53, 59, 87, 131, 151, 212
Leads, 123, 189, 208, 214
Letters, 208, 239, 251, 253
Lifetime value of clients, 53, 88, 144, 180, 201, 228, 263, 264, 266
Living Trust, 132
Logo, 63, 73, 123, 138, 149, 157, 160, 182, 241

M&M's, 46, 59, 75
Magazines, 12, 30, 74, 91, 95, 101, 111, 131, 134, 160, 163, 164, 167, 168, 173, 175, 180, 193
Magic bullets, 11, 12
Marketing consultant, xiii, xiv, xv, xvi, xvii, 3, 7, 12, 26, 34, 35, 36, 39, 49, 59, 77, 78, 81, 93, 96, 103, 107, 111, 133, 147, 156, 159, 172, 191, 211, 221
Marketing mindset, 15, 16, 17, 35, 229
Marketing Planner, 233
McDonald's, 7, 47, 266
Meetings, 252, 259
Meetup.com, 84
Microsoft, 96, 163
Mobile, 29, 211, 213, 215, 223, 228
Montgomery Ward, 77
Morabito, Joseph, 159, 190, 259

Networking, 83, 84
Newsletters, 234
Newspapers, 12, 74, 85, 91, 92, 96, 113, 123, 131, 132, 138, 144, 163, 167, 169, 175, 180, 193, 259
Nicholas, Ted, vii, 131, 133, 134, 164, 166

Offer, 125, 137, 139, 208, 252
Ogilvy and Mather, 167

Ogilvy, David, 93, 97, 107, 129, 167, 168
Operations, 21, 25

Paragon Global Resources, 159
PC Magazine, 30
Pinterest, 85
Plumbers, 111, 139, 212
Postcards, 140, 206, 208
Price, 50, 126
Proof, 125
Psychographics, 108

Quality, 26, 29, 33, 47, 50, 75, 181, 207, 255, 261

Radio, 33, 62, 66, 68, 85, 101, 111, 116, 122, 123, 130, 144, 175, 180, 259
Real estate agents, 63, 109, 113, 122, 139, 214, 244
Reebok, 158
Reeves, Rosser, 45, 46, 269
Referrals, 195, 197, 198, 248
Retail stores, 25, 42, 44, 47, 48, 77, 95, 126, 137, 140, 175, 193, 201, 207, 212
Rolls-Royce, 168
Ron Paul Curriculum, xiv, 42, 152, 153, 226

Schwab, Victor, 119, 121, 125, 129, 141, 143, 157, 163, 269
Sears, 77
SEO, 216
Service professionals, 138, 139, 212
Settle, Ben, 243
Simplicity Homes, 198
Smartphone, 33
Solution, 121, 124, 127
Staff, xvi, xviii, 24, 25, 29, 31, 33, 35, 54, 60, 68, 197, 207, 212, 217, 224, 248

Taco Bell, 96
Target, 47

Television, 68, 85, 95, 131, 149,
    175, 180, 192
Testimonials, 43, 53, 54, 61, 78,
    104, 120, 121, 124, 125, 133,
    165, 208, 212, 213, 217, 223,
    248, 256, 264
The Wall Street Journal, 117, 131,
    165
Time, xiv, xv, xviii, 3, 11, 12, 16,
    17, 19, 21, 22, 23, 25, 26, 27,
    29, 31, 32, 34, 35, 42, 43, 62,
    68, 77, 81, 83, 85, 88, 97, 111,
    112, 114, 116, 121, 123, 125, 133,
    149, 173, 190, 195, 201, 206,
    210, 213, 225, 226, 229, 235,
    237, 238, 239, 244, 245, 253,
    255, 259, 260, 265, 267
Toastmasters, 84, 176, 181, 275
Twitter, 20, 243
Typology, 153

Unique, 47, 61, 240, 265
United Airlines, 47
USP, 9, 39, 43, 45, 49, 57, 59, 61,

66, 67, 73, 77, 81, 89, 126, 137,
    171, 174, 187, 196, 208, 212,
    214, 223, 227, 237, 247, 251,
    265

Vacations, 134, 192, 227
Video, 44, 220
Volkswagen, 96

Walmart, 5, 39, 41, 47, 73, 77,
    116, 214
Walt Disney, 41
Website, 62, 70, 209, 216, 223
Website Builders, 225, 226, 229
WII-FM, 101, 119, 130, 131, 148,
    216, 218, 228
Wonder Bread, 46
WordPress, 203, 219, 225, 230

Yellow Pages, 138, 163, 175, 180,
    194

Ziglar, Zig, 25, 26, 87, 88

About the Author

Richard Emmons' first business was selling candy bars to his elementary school classmates during the lunch hour in 6th grade. Sadly, his business got shut down by a government official, his teacher.

Richard attended the U.S. Naval Academy for two years, realized life as a naval officer would not float his boat, so he moved back to California to graduate from California State University Fullerton with an accounting degree.

He began his career in corporate finance and became the controller of a Weyerhaeuser subsidiary at age 28. Two years later he helped spinoff this company in a leveraged buy-out. As the Chief Financial Officer, he oversaw accounting, administration, and IT.

Richard has over 25 years of senior management experience in six different industry sectors including financial services, real estate, relocation services, banking, research and development, and light manufacturing. His sales experience includes business-to-business direct sales and door-to-door selling to homeowners and businesses. He now works with business owners and professionals to help them maximize their business growth success through coaching, consulting, and office management services.

Richard began studying nontraditional marketing principles with Jay Abraham's Protégé Mentor program in 1989. He continues to feed his voracious appetite for information on marketing and business success. A Toastmaster for many years, Richard never misses an opportunity to promote this proven and practical organization. Toastmasters.org.

Richard created a business course for the Ron Paul Curriculum. In 180 video-based lessons, he teaches students to plan and launch an online business during their high school years. HighSchoolBiz.com.

Richard enjoys living in Southern Oregon with his wife and family. Learn more about his books and services at richardemmons.com.